P9-CEH-062

No Place Like Hope

No Place Like Hope

A journey through poverty

STANLEY LEONE JR.

© 2017 Stanley Leone Jr.
All rights reserved.

ISBN-13: 9780692931806
ISBN-10: 0692931805
Library of Congress Control Number: 2017951282
Press On, Smithtown, NY

Contents

There have been countless people who have impacted my life up until this point but none so much as Cheryl and Rachel. Thank you both for the years of love and support and for always believing I could do this.

Preface

It was a very difficult process in coming up with this material through interviews, memories, and secondhand stories from both sides of the family. I have done my best to portray my early childhood as well as paint an honest picture of the four men I met as an adult: my father and uncles Henry, Wayne, and Jared, along with their families.

Try as I might, there will always be a degree of variation in perspective and the way individuals remember stories. Please take into account that there are 3 major obstacles I am attempting to overcome. First, I was a kid when these things happened with my father, and naturally the perspective of a child will always be different than that of an adult. Second, I'm working from memories, my own as well as that of the individuals interviewed, that are at least 25 years old.

Finally, I have tried to accurately represent the language used during that time in my life, as well as the language used by my uncles during our conversations. Because I now find such language offensive I have done what I am able to minimize the offensiveness by not spelling certain words out, and substituting where possible. This is my attempt to prevent the language from getting in the way of the message.

Given these factors, I believe I have written with deliberate honesty, protecting some whose stories are not mine to tell and revealing others who are directly involved with my own story. My hope is to use my experiences to bring some good into the world.

Live on purpose,
Stanley Leone Jr.

One

In the Beginning

*Life is thickly sown with thorns, and I know no other remedy
than to pass quickly through them. The longer we dwell on
our misfortunes, the greater is their power to harm us.*

—Voltaire

Against a dimly lit backdrop with a hip-hop song signaling the start of
my presentation, I step on stage. In baggy jeans, muscle shirt, and
knit cap, I look just like any other kid from my neighborhood.

As I begin my presentation, I pace back and forth across the stage
like a caged animal. I appear fearless but am afraid, arrogant but insecure, composed but explosive, and it would all be accurate. I am all
those things.

"Guess it was bad from the start, wasn't it, Dad?" I ask loudly, con-
fronting a father who exists now only in my memory. Suddenly, I shout,
in a voice thick with rage and pain. "You thought I forgot? I remember
three times! Three times you tried to murder my mom! You tried to take
her out of my life! Three times! And you thought I forgot?"

The audience sit rapt. I can hear them breathing on the second row in the second level. My heart is pounding, and a thousand thoughts rush through my head.

I'm no longer that scared little boy—except when I'm on stage. For years, I have been donning my childhood persona to reenact—and often even relive—some of the most traumatic events of my life.

There is silence. I'm no longer the confrontational boy—angry and violent. My voice becomes small and timid.

"Daddy, please don't hurt her. I'm scared, Daddy. I don't want Mommy to die! Please!" My words echo with the agony of a child who has seen unspeakable abuse perpetrated against the people he loves the most.

My demeanor changes again. The timid boy becomes the angry teen.

"But there wasn't any comfort from you, Dad," I say disdainfully. "You come over, and I get hit. *Bam!* 'You don't cry for no women, boy! You be strong like your father! You be a man like your daddy, boy! See, we don't weep over no women, kid!'"

This is my story. It's the story of an abused child, troubled teen, and determined adult struggling to overcome a family legacy of violence, addiction, and abuse. It is a story that I've shared onstage with hundreds of thousands of students and teachers across the nation who have found it captivating, heartbreaking, and inspirational. It is the story I was written into, and while it brings others hope, it fills me with dread. Every time I tell it.

By the time I was not much older than 5, the nightmares had already begun.

I remember playing in those days, running down a cracked, tar-stained street, full of life and energy, full of hope and promise. My hair was always a messy chocolate brown, disheveled and plastered to my forehead, in part because of the sweat and in part the humidity. But those playful outings always turned into anxious nights. It was better for us to be outside than it was to be home. Our apartment was a place hope went to die.

I raced home one day after school, excited to share my good news with Mom. I turned a corner lined with prickly green bushes, the kind that draw blood if they poke you, and then I jumped a yellow-striped painted curb and landed on the courtyard lawn in front of my apartment. I bolted forward and flung the paint-chipped door open and vanished as the door closed behind me.

"Mom, are you home?" I shrieked.

"I'm in the kitchen!" she yelled back.

Choppy steps carried me through the living room, and I stumbled into the undersized and cluttered kitchen and fell into my mom's arms, squeezing her tightly. She pretended she was happy to see me.

"Mom, Mom. Guess what? I got an A on my spelling. See!" I stretched out my quivering hand, gripping a single page of slightly crumpled notebook paper with the letter A sprawled across the top margin.

"Look, Mom. It's an A! I got an A! Ms. Boccarosa said I did really good." I smiled expectantly, eagerly anticipating her response.

"That's good," she replied indifferently, bacon grease splattering across her shirt and onto the floor. "Go change your clothes, and go outside with your brothers."

She turned her petite frame away from me to face the stove and resumed frying her popping bacon. The pan bubbled with fat, the stove simmered with heat, and the apartment filled with the aroma of charred pork and the stench of my disappointment. My smile slowly lost its lift, curling into the definite twist of a heartbroken frown. I dropped my head as my shoulders slumped, turned, and allowed my feet to shuffle me into my bedroom. I changed my clothes and joined my brothers outside, forgetting the A I'd been so proud of. Disappointment washed away the hope and joy I'd come home with.

Several hours of roughhousing and playing chase left us tired and hungry when we finally fell into the apartment. We burst in, flooding the place with laughter. I tagged my older brother on the shoulder and then turned to run. He reached out and grabbed my leg, and the three of us went falling and tumbling and slipping and sliding as we spilled one then the other and another into the living room and onto the floor.

"You're it!" shouted Johnny, my oldest brother.

"No, you're it!" I shouted back.

"You both can't catch me," shouted Bo, our youngest brother, and he dashed toward the kitchen and the safety of dinner, a sly grin on his lips.

Mom stood by the vinyl-topped kitchen table, her hands on her hips, digging into rough, sun-dried skin. Brows furrowed, she looked at us, dirty and sweaty from the daylong retreat outdoors. I walked to the dinner table and got slapped behind the head before I could take a seat.

Mom pointed at the chairs and said in a cold, quiet voice, "Shut up, and get your asses to the table."

All three of us knew better than to disobey. We sucked in our breath, our eyes wide, and we choked on the thick air in the room. We lowered our heads and meekly sought our places around the table. Spaghetti sat fat, wet, and red in the scratched and dinged silver pot that rested front and center. I eyed the stringy, gloppy mess, and it seemed to stare back. Finally, uneasiness began to grow in the pit of my gut, like the sickness that comes from drinking spoiled milk, and I turned my head and averted my eyes. That's when I saw my father sitting in his old recliner in the living room. *We must have stumbled right past him,* I thought, kicking myself.

He was drinking lukewarm beer, watching some insignificant show on our rickety TV. It was going to be a typical night, and we all tensed. There were no family meals in our house. Just kids at the table, Dad in his chair, and Mom in the kitchen busying herself with the business of nothing. I shifted my eyes back to the spaghetti. It was still staring at me.

Without preamble we all began to eat. You wouldn't hear conversations at our table. The safest thing was for the scraping of forks on plastic to be the only sounds made. We knew better than to disrupt the traditional awkward silence that had become the norm or intrude on the distant thoughts of parents who thought nothing and wanted nothing. We simply ate until the spaghetti was all gone, and then we rose from folding chairs and placed our bowls in the overfilled sink. No one said a word. No one made eye contact, and no one smiled. Night enveloped the silence-filled apartment, and we disappeared down the short hallway.

My wide eyes scanned up and down as I passed through the smudged, cracked hallway littered with torn and faded photographs, taken with cheap film in cheap cameras. The sounds of yelling emanated from the twenty-seven-inch TV in the living room, rattling the bunny-eared, foil-tipped antenna and crackling the aged internal speakers. It was a good night. There was no crying, no hitting, no slapping, no yelling, no cussing, no bleeding, and no beating. It *was* a good night...so far.

I knew my father was not happy, and my mother wasn't either, but that wasn't unusual. *Happy* didn't visit the projects. It spent all its time in neighborhoods with moms who packed lunches and dads who tucked their kids in at night. Those neighborhoods were a long ways away from mine. I heard the bathroom door closing quietly as the sound seemed to whisper through the darkened hallway. I reached for the dirty silver doorknob of our bedroom door and turned it. Without looking back, we disappeared into the room silently, secretly. Roaches scattered when I turned on the light.

"Do you think they'll fight tonight?" I asked my brother, pleading for assurance.

"I don't know. Dad was only drinking beer. It's usually the other stuff that makes him mean," said Johnny.

"But they were mad. I know it," I countered.

"Just keep quiet, and don't give them a reason to come in here, and we'll be OK," he replied.

"But I don't want Daddy to hit Mom again. I don't want him to hit her, not again," I sobbed.

Johnny looked on, sadness clouding his eyes. "I know, buddy. It'll be OK. Let's just get some sleep, and they'll be OK. Dad looked sleepy, so maybe he'll pass out before he gets mean."

Tears slipped from pools that swelled in the corners of my eyes, slid down the slope of my nose, and dribbled into my mouth. I licked my lips and tasted the saltiness of sadness, silently sobbed, and said, "I just don't want him to hit her no more. I just don't."

Johnny slowly slugged toward me, wrapped his meaty arms around my skinny neck, and pulled me into his chest, whispering, "Me neither." Bo huddled close at my waist.

The room was small, so I guess it goes without saying that everything else in the room was as well. There was a twin-sized mattress atop a box spring against the wall nearest to the door. Directly across on the opposite wall were the windows we would sometimes look out to watch the crazy things that happened at night. The closet was against the wall on the right and a small, plywood dresser sat to the left.

Even at that age, I knew that our apartment was dirty. It didn't seem like a big deal because we were always dirty too, so the unit suited us. I shuffled toward the front-right corner where I slept and lay on rumpled sheets piled on the dirty floor. I lifted the oldest of the thinning sheets and slithered my skinny legs underneath, feeling the dampness of muddy carpet as I slid my feet across the floor. I rested my head against my pillow and could feel the hard floor beneath.

Some people might be uncomfortable on that floor, but not me. I'd grown used to it. The wetness of the sticky carpet and the assurance of the worn, dingy pillow had become symbols of peace and comfort. If I was able to make it to my room without Dad hitting someone or throwing something, that usually meant we'd have an uneventful night. By that time in my life, all I wanted was uneventful. I laid my head low and felt my breathing slow. A pulsating throb slammed into my skull, and I wrapped my hands around my head and tried to sleep, grateful for the distraction of another headache.

I inhaled. And released. Inhaled. Exhaled. My head throbbed. Inhaled and exhaled again. Still throbbing. But I was at peace. My mother was OK. Thoughts filled my mind and swam through the chambers of my pounding head, spinning and twisting and winding in and out, circling one another, crashing into the walls of my aching brain. But still I was at peace. My eyes finally drooped, heavy with relaxation. Heavy with tension

6

and fear and pain. They were heavy, and they drooped, and I slept in the best kind of peace I knew—silence.

"Stop it! Please don't hit me. Stop!" came the terrified shouts of a woman, her voice a series of wheezes.

I sat up, startled, peace stripped away. *Oh no, it's happening again*, I thought out loud. I was alert and afraid and angry, and I felt completely alone. I knew my brothers were there, but I did not ask them if they heard the screams. I knew they had. I remember feeling angry. I feel the anger swelling up inside of me even now. So angry. My breathing squeezed through tightly contracting lungs, rasping and wheezing as it came. I sat erect and listened, and I was so damn mad—and deathly afraid!

Why can't he just let her be? I wondered.

The cries and gurgles and pants drifted softly against the walls and stung my eyes until they were wet with sorrow. Standing slowly, tiptoeing slowly, and breathing slowly, I silently approached the door in the darkness and twisted the cold metal knob. I leaned forward slightly to peak through the crack, when a big, bulging, brown eye peered through the breech, and I fell back on my rear. It was my mother, and she was hurt, reaching for the knob that I'd just twisted while my dad hit her. His hands exploded into her face. I could see that her neck was hurt, and she lay on her back on the floor. My dad straddled her and clutched his violent hands around her neck.

"Please," wheezed my mom. "I can't breathe. You're hurting me."

Slowly, holding my breath, I jumped back to my feet and slammed the door shut. I don't know why I did it. I guess I could say, if I wanted to be poetic about it, that closing the door was my attempt to shut everything out. The truth is, I was terrified, and I didn't want my dad to turn his attention to us. I carefully returned to my rumpled sheets and laid on my back, straightened myself by locking my knees, and I endured the blows I heard crashing one after the other upon my mother. Crash. Endure. Thump. Endure. Smash. Endure some more.

Heaviness. Sorrow. Grief. We felt all these things, but my brothers and I did not speak for fear of being heard and causing our father to

7

turn on us. I lay alone, and in my loneliness, I longed to fall thoughtlessly into the ever-after of dreams that were not dreams. I was desperate to escape into the land of other worlds and make-believe. Trembling, my teeth chattering, I squeezed my eyes shut and wrapped my shaky arms around my sticklike legs, pulling them into my bony chest. I smothered the sobs by pressing dirty hands to my mouth, and I rocked ever so subtly to the sounds of my mom's mumbled cries, and I drifted halfway between here and somewhere else. Somewhere, anywhere, far and farther away, and I longed to just disappear.

I was grateful for the darkness of the night because it made it easier to feel like I wasn't there, in that apartment and on that floor. My mother's screams echoed through empty halls and fell on empty ears, and finally I did sleep, though it was not a peaceful sleep, not a restful sleep, but one that leaves you exhausted in the morning, filled with the troubles that come with an abused mother, in a violent family, from a broken home. But I slept nonetheless.

Two

My Mom, the Hero

Some of us weren't born for rewards...
We were born for sacrifices.

—Melina Marchetta, *Froi of the Exiles*

Mom woke us in the morning, as usual. She was embarrassed and angry.

"Get your asses up!" she yelled, throwing the door open. "You're going to be late for school!"

I pushed the sheet off me and rolled to my knees on the floor. Mom was standing in the hallway with the door opened far enough for me to see her. She looked miserable. There were bruises around her neck, and the right side of her face was swollen black, purple, and blue. Her right eye was bloodshot. I averted my eyes, staring at the floor instead, and rose to my feet. When I glanced back a few moments later, she was gone.

We went to school that day and pretended like nothing happened. I take that back; I didn't pretend because somehow I was able to miraculously forget that the whole event occurred. I still remember losing myself in grade-level math competitions. I would engross myself so deeply that

I actually won a few times, despite the fact that I never got over doing multiplication on my fingers.

Gym was where I found I could excel the most. If we were riding scooter boards, I was working out how best to reverse directions so that I'd win, pushing myself back to the opposite baseboard. If it was the get-fit test, I'd go last so I knew how far to stretch, how many push-ups and pull-ups to do. I'd say it was early in my life that I discovered that people liked winners, and my identity began to develop around whether I won or lost.

I'd say I was a good winner because I was happy when it happened, and I never wanted others to feel bad; I just wanted them to like me. To think I was good at something. To want me on their team. Without a doubt I was a bad loser. I'd fight people, kick the basketball into the parking lot, accuse others of cheating, or grow violent while we played. When I lost, it wasn't as if I stopped thinking about it when the game was over. It stayed with me for days, sometimes weeks, like a serpent twisting in my gut when I recalled the defeat.

I made a valiant effort to deal with it, telling myself things like, *He's bigger than you*, or *Just practice more, and you'll beat him*, but it never worked. Each time I tried to convince myself that losing was OK, or that there was a way to win next time, I was always brought back to the fact that I'd lost *that time*. An overwhelming feeling would nearly cripple me or drive me to outbursts of rage, when my reasoning turned to things like, *You'll never beat someone who's bigger than you*, or *What if you practice the rest of your life and you're still not good enough?*

I understand now that the fear of not being able to beat someone who was bigger than me was deeper than sports; it was about my dad and the fear that I would never be able to stand up to him. I also understand that the fear that I would never be good enough was tied to both my dad and my mom and the sense that I was unlovable. I understand all of that... *now*.

But as a child, I was forced to internalize those things, without a clue that I was doing it or the tools to do it with. Thinking about it now reminds me of the time I was thrown into the deep end of the pool because I told my mom's boyfriend I couldn't swim. He told me, "There's only one way to learn," and tossed me into the water.

I sank at first but didn't know I was sinking. My eyes were closed, cheeks puffed with air, and I could feel the strands of my hair floating up from my head. It wasn't until I opened my eyes, I don't know how much later, that I realized I was nearly touching the bottom of a ten-foot pool. I panicked, threw my arms every which way, but didn't go anywhere. When I touched the concrete, I pushed off with all my might, clawed upward at the water, and broke the surface, gulping in as much air as I could. I kicked my feet, because that's what I'd seen the other kids do, and slapped at the water and was able to make it to the side, where I pulled myself out.

It's the same thing when kids are forced to swim in the deep waters of poverty. They have no idea that they are sinking; they just know they have to do something, and that something is always what they've seen. It's always what they've learned. My father hit my mother, he hit other people, when he was angry, so that's what I did. My mother cussed and belittled me when she was angry, so that's what I did. Kids kick and slap at the water and gulp at whatever air they can get, even if the air they're breathing is toxic.

There were many more nights like the one I described, and each time my brothers and I would cower in the room and hope that my father didn't turn on us. Don't get me wrong; he beat us, but only when he was sober, and we were grateful for that. Breathing in that toxic air.

My mom, on the other hand, had it bad. He only attacked her when he was drunk. I could get extremely graphic here, about when he raped my mother, and how he tortured her, but I won't. I will share that there were three times when I thought he'd kill her. Most of the time we hoped he wouldn't kill her, but on those three occasions, there was nothing to hope for. We knew she would die.

The first time happened on a Saturday morning. My brother and I woke to screaming in the kitchen. Johnny grabbed me by the shirt and put his finger to his lips. He pulled me behind him into the hallway, and we peaked around the corner. We could hear my father screaming and my mother sobbing.

"Leave it," demanded Dad. "You better not touch that damn thing. You can take it out when I tell you to."

"Please, Stan," begged Mom. "Baby, I'm sorry. I didn't do nothing; please, it hurts me."

"You filthy whore," screamed Dad, "you think you can sleep with other men and I won't find out!" He grunted.

Mom whined. "Please, I didn't sleep with anyone!" she cried. "I don't know why you think that. I don't do nothing but sit in this apartment and look after things for you." She was shouting now. "It's hurting me, Stan!"

My brother and I crept through the living room until we were nearly in the sitting area of the kitchen, and we could see around the short wall that separated the dining area from the living room. Mom was squatting on the floor, reaching forward with trembling hands, attempting to pull the steak knife out of her foot. Dad had just returned from being out at the bars all night, stinking drunk, and from the moment he stepped into the apartment, he'd begun accusing Mom of cheating on him. Not convinced by her denials, he grabbed a steak knife off the counter and stabbed her in the foot with it.

Once I was able to pull my eyes from Mom, and the blood, I saw that Dad had a kitchen drawer pulled open. His hand was holding a spoon, and when my mother reached for the knife again, he flung it at her, hitting her with such force in the shoulder that her skin went instantly red. We were terrified when Mom started talking to us.

"Babies, go back to the room."

Dad looked at us, we held our breath, and he dropped the spoon, turned, grabbed his beer from the table, and then walked past us into the living room and plopped into his recliner, where he passed out.

We left him that day. Mom packed us up, and we fled to Louisiana to stay with John, my mom's father. We'd already run to my grandmother and step-grandfather on several occasions, and they'd given my mom an ultimatum the last time we were there. Either we stay with them or we stay with Stan, but they wouldn't be a part of the back and forth. So we went to her dad's instead. He was never a grandpa to me, or to any of us. Staying with him lasted a day.

There weren't enough rooms for us to sleep, so that night, John, my grandfather, asked Bo to sleep with him. I don't know how I knew this because at that time I didn't know anything about my mom's relationship with John, but there was something in the way he asked Bo to sleep in his room that I didn't like, or trust.

"I'll sleep here," I said, pressing my hand against Bo's chest and pushing him back.

Bo stepped away, and Mom grabbed him, looked at me, and then looked at her father.

"Come on, sweetie; let's go to bed."

They left the room, and John told me to turn off the light. I did what he said.

"Come on, boy; come get in this bed," he said in the darkness.

I walked to the bed slowly, my eyes adjusted to the night, and saw his silhouette holding the blanket back. I climbed in bed and laid on my back while he pulled the blanket up to my chin.

"Why don't you cuddle with your grandpa?" he whispered.

He must have turned on his side because he placed a hand on my shoulder and rolled me over until my back faced him. He put his arm around me and pulled himself close. I closed my eyes so that I wouldn't know I was sinking.

A brightness flashed across my eyelids, and when I opened my eyes, my mother, my beautiful savior of a mother, was standing in the doorway, one hand on the knob, the other on the light switch, staring hard into the room.

"Come on, Junior," she said. "You're sleeping with me tonight."

I threw the cover off me, clambered out of the bed, and ran to my mom, pushing my face into her hip and hugging her leg. We walked out, the door slamming shut behind us. The next day we returned to my father.

My brothers and I had often wondered why Mom didn't just leave Dad. We'd run from him several times, but she always chose to go back. When I look at her situation now, I think it was a matter of experience. All Mom had known her entire life was dependency on men. She'd fled from her father at fourteen, when she could no longer deal with the rapes and his declarations that she "wasn't his daughter anyway, so it was all right." Her escape was a young, handsome boy not much older than her.

Not long after she was pregnant with my older brother, whom she had at sixteen. She soon found herself alone when the boy she was in love with realized he was too young to be a father. Mom did what she knew: she sought another man to take care of her and found my father. From the very beginning, my mother had fallen into a cycle of dependence, and the people she depended on lived in the same poverty as her. It's important to note that the poverty I speak of has nothing, or at least very little to do with, money. Poverty is a distortion of value systems, a survival-based value system that breeds pain and dysfunction.

Mom didn't know she could go to shelters or seek out assistance from churches. She had no idea she could go to one of our schools to get help from the principal. So in truth, for my mother, it wasn't that she made bad choices; it was that, for *her*, she only had bad choices. That's how poverty works. A person is so consumed by the dysfunction that every decision becomes a short-term response to escape it.

I also realize that that night my mom was a hero. She saved me. I know it now, and I knew it then, even if I wasn't allowed to talk about it or to thank her for interceding. I knew she'd saved me from something awful. To this day that night stands out in my mind as one of the few times in my childhood when I knew without a doubt that someone thought I was worth saving. Thank you mom.

Three

A Violent Lesson

*The most benevolent souls are the ones who have had
to drink some of life's worst poisons, yet protected others
in their lives from ever having to taste them.*

—Jose N. Harris

It was a couple of weeks before the next time Dad nearly killed my mom. Johnny woke me early in the morning. There was screaming again—*that* wasn't different—but what was unusual was that we only heard Dad. Mom didn't make a sound.

"Dad's mad about something," he whispered, turning to look at me.

"At least they're not arguing again," I replied, my eyes locked on him for confirmation. "Should we go out there?"

My brother glanced at the door and thought for a moment. "Yeah," he confirmed, "but stay behind me."

I nodded my agreement as he opened the door, and we stepped into the hallway. Dad's voice hit us with a barrage of swear words, and I ducked instinctively. Johnny turned and put his finger to his lips. His eyes were hard as stone, as though he knew what we'd find before we got there. The sounds were coming from the kitchen again.

We tiptoed as quietly as we could, my hand pressed against the wall to keep me steady, and I followed closely behind my brother. I watched him carefully and was in awe of how broad he was even then. He was ten years old, but while I was a skinny kid, he was thick and big boned. I always felt so safe with him. His long, curly blond hair tussled shoulder length with each step, his shoulders wide and hard. Even from behind him, I could see that he was tense, his hands gripped into fists, his jaw clenched tightly.

The smell of sulfuric blood and alcohol hit me when we entered the living room. It seemed to waft up from the floor and loiter in the air, probing at my nostrils as we stepped into the fog of it.

"You filthy whore," rang out shouts from the kitchen, "I'll kill you before I let you make a fool of me. I'm out working my ass off, and you're home all day, smiling at these bitch-ass Mexicans and spreading your legs for them!"

Johnny reached back and placed his hand on my chest as we neared the wall that separated the kitchen from the living room, and we slowed. Each step was tentative, as though we were stepping out of time and into somewhere in between now and then. My pulse raced, but even the sound of it in my head slowed and seemed to labor with each beat. Johnny took another step until at last we could see what my father had created.

The kitchen tile was crimson, a large puddle, the size of a bathtub, spread along the floor and encircled a motionless body. Mom lay still, face down, her hair tangled in a bloody mess, her hands pressed palms down in the red puddle. She was wearing a pair of my brother's gym shorts and a gray T-shirt, and her bare feet sat against the floor, like a hatchet buried in chopping wood.

Dad hovered over her, shirtless, his chest heaving in and out heavily, his face a mask of rage. He snarled when he saw us.

"Get your asses back to your room!" he shouted dangerously.

I turned to go, hesitating for a moment to wait for Johnny, but when he did not move, I remained still, my body turned halfway toward the room. I watched as his hands clenched harder into tightly bound fists.

"Get away from her."

He didn't shout, but his voice didn't waiver either. It was steady and threatening. My heart skipped a beat. I glanced over my shoulder and saw flames begin to lick in my father's eyes. He squared up with my brother, the broom handle he'd broken over my mother's head still clasped tightly in his hand.

"What did you say to me?"

My mouth went dry. I reached forward and tugged at Johnny's hand, pulling him slightly, but he pulled his fist away from my grip and took another step forward.

"I said, get away from my mother."

It happened so fast I didn't realize what was going on until I heard Johnny's garbled screams emanating from the bathroom. Dad had taken a step forward, Johnny lashed out with his fist, and I fell to the floor, covering my ears and screaming. I don't remember what I was saying, or if I was even really saying anything. I just knew I didn't want to be there, so I closed my eyes and made my own noise to drown out the sounds of the present. When I stopped shouting is when I heard his.

"Don't," wailed Johnny, "please, sto—"

"You piece of shit," accused my dad, "you want to raise your hand to me."

I rose to my feet and sprinted along the hallway, turned left, and entered the bathroom. I heard the water, like a freight train, flooding the bathtub, and the sounds of splashing, and then gurgles. I pushed my way through the doorway and found Dad kneeling next to the bathtub, his hand gripping a wad of my brother's curly blond locks, holding his head beneath the water.

Johnny was fully clothed, one hand pressed tightly to my dad's wrist, the other pressed flat against the bathroom tile on the wall. Water splashed into every direction as he kicked furiously to free himself. I leaned forward and saw his panicked wide eyes, and his mouth shouting beneath the water. Without thinking I screamed and lunged at my dad.

"Stop it!" I cried, slamming both of my skinny hands into his face. "Leave him alone!" I closed my eyes and struck at him as quickly and with as much force as I could.

I don't know how long I hit him, but when I opened my eyes, exhausted from crying and tired from hitting him, Johnny was sitting in the tub with his back against the wall. The water still rushed from the pipe, and Dad still remained kneeling. His face looked sunken, sadness replacing the fury, and without a word he reached for the water nozzles and shut them off. Silently he rose and left us.

"Are you OK?" I sniffled. The front door opened and slammed shut.

Johnny's eyes followed the sound. "I'm fine," he said, biting down on his jaw again. "Let's go check on Mom."

When we returned to the kitchen, Mom remained in the same position we'd last seen her.

Emotion stirred in me, and I could not contain my tears. "Is she dead?" I cried, my breaths coming in gasps.

Johnny stared down. "She's breathing," he said, emotionless, grabbing a pot from the dish rack and then filling it up with water from the faucet. I stood by and watched as he hauled the filled pot over to where our mother lay and then dumped it on her face.

Mom stirred, moving her head away from the splash, completely unaware of where she was or what had happened. Johnny set the pot on the sink and leaned over her, placing both hands on her shoulders.

"You're OK, Mom," he whispered oddly, still without emotion. "Come on," he said. "We need to get you help." He turned to me. "We need to get her up."

I was of absolutely no help to him. I was not a strong kid, and even though I tried as much as I could, I could not lift my mother. I pulled and tugged but only seemed to get in the way. Johnny turned and motioned me back, and then I watched this ten-year-old heave our mother onto his back and haul her into the bathroom. I stood in awe as I watched him strain beneath her weight, her feet dragging along the floor behind him.

I went into the bedroom and woke up Bo and brought him to the bathroom where Johnny had Mom. We washed the blood from her body. The entire right side of her face was covered with wet cloths, and then Johnny pulled her into the bedroom and laid her on the bed. She was in and out of consciousness, sometimes waking up confused about where she was, other times muttering, "He's going to kill me," or "I didn't do nothing," but Johnny pressed on with what he was doing until finally she was dressed and more presentable.

He left Bo and me in the room while he ran around the apartment until he returned with Mom's car keys a few moments later. "Come on," he said to us, standing Mom up and allowing her to fall onto his back again. We followed as he carried her outside, through the parking lot, and loaded her into the passenger side of the car. "Get in."

Johnny drove us to the free clinic in Pasadena and got my mom into the emergency room. He told the nurse that Mom had fallen and busted her head open on the counter. That day they used seventeen staples to close the wound my father had opened along her skull. We had learned a valuable lesson: none of us were safe.

Four

THE LITTLE TRAIN THAT COULD

Desperation is the raw material of drastic change. Only those
who can leave behind everything…can hope to escape.

—WILLIAM S. BURROUGHS

It's hard to remember what life was like during my formative years. Most of the memories seem to be overshadowed by the constant fear we lived in. In spite of those more painful experiences, there are some memories that I think fondly of. I remember the hours my brothers and I spent outside and the incredible games we used to play. It seemed like life was perfect when we were playing tag, hide-and-seek, duck, duck, goose, or any of a dozen or so other things to kill the time.

But one of my favorite memories took place indoors. There were days when it rained and we weren't allowed to leave our room. It was during those times that we'd discovered the joys of creating forts. The single dresser we had would serve as the foundation of what would be the safest place in our lives. We'd slide the dresser out from the wall just enough to be able to drape a sheet over the top. Then we'd pull the sheet free, just a bit, and pin down the corners with anything heavy we could find: shoes, books, toys. Next we took pillows and lined them along the insides of the sheet so that, once inside, we sat in the middle of a nearly perfect square.

It seems silly now, but I remember how excited I was about that fort. When we'd first built it, we'd fallen asleep inside making up stories about monsters that surrounded us, hovering and waiting to gobble us up but unable to penetrate the walls of our fort. Those were some of the best nights of sleep we had prior to leaving my father.

I think it's important to note that it doesn't take much to give a child hope when he or she is in a desperate situation. It is amazing what types of things we'll cling to in order to survive. My older brother, a sheet, a pile of pillows, and an old dresser were enough to provide sanctuary, despite the fact that we lived in a daily hell. When it wasn't the fort, it was the random games we played outside. At times it was something as simple as a good grade in school, a compliment from a teacher, or a kind gesture from a sacker in a grocery store.

As an adult I'm grateful for those small *things*...but I can't help but wonder how much more impactful it is if kids have *people* rather than things to cling to. There is no replacement for a relationship. It's incredible to me that with everything that went on in my life at that time that there wasn't one adult who intervened on our behalf. How is it possible that three kids could experience such trauma and yet go virtually unnoticed by anyone willing to help?

What happens to kids when they don't have a big brother like I did? What happens to those big brothers? The day my mother was beaten unconscious with a broom handle was a day that changed my brother forever. I think that was the first time I'd seen him emotionally detach. Although his actions were kind, they were performed with no compassion. Even an act as caring as cleaning our bloodied mother was done in a businesslike manner. That detachment went on to affect Johnny well into his adult years, making intimacy in relationships difficult for him. To this day, now past forty, Johnny struggles with a *survivor* mentality, poverty, and it prevents the vulnerability that relationships require. He's been blessed enough to find a wife who understands him and children who love him, and he lives a good life despite these struggles. What are the consequences when there are no relationships? What are the consequences for kids who have no connection with an appropriate adult?

I was lucky in that sense. I've had numerous adults play active roles throughout my life. Although I consider myself a healthy adult, so much of who we are is wired in those formative years, and the effects of dysfunctional wiring early on has a dramatic impact on who we are and the lives we lead. From the start I was being taught that there are two kinds of people in the world: perpetrators and victims. If life is a game, my father was wiring me with the rules he knew. Rule number one: You hurt people, or they hurt you. There is no in-between. Rule number two: We're not built for relationships because the closer you get to people, the more power you give them to hurt you. I consider myself a quick learner, and I quickly learned the rules and played the game.

I identified with my mother, and so, like her, I was a victim. I learned early on that I couldn't make things happen, that things happened to me. Strangely enough, I also learned that people didn't truly love you until they hurt you. The sense that I was unworthy of a love without abuse overwhelmed me well into my adult years, and the belief that I deserved to be loved at all was the most difficult obstacle to overcome.

As I grew up and got bigger, I recognized that with my newfound strength and size I could graduate, so to speak, and assume the role of perpetrator. Although I hated my father, there would eventually be a time in my life when I looked just like him, behaved like him, and most likely thought like him. But that's for a later time.

Home had quieted down. Mom didn't talk much when she'd returned from the clinic with her head stapled, and Dad didn't hit her. He'd still drink, still get drunk, but more times than not, other than a few insults and accusations, he didn't harass Mom the way he'd done in the past. I'm not saying that things were good—not by a long shot—but they *were* better.

Johnny had grown quiet as well. Where before he was attentive and overly protective, he'd grown distant and withdrawn with us. On the occasions I saw him at school, he seemed louder, more outgoing than ever, quick to laugh, even quicker to make others laugh, but never quite himself. We no longer played outside together. Johnny had begun hanging out with other kids, and he stayed away from home until well into the evenings, when he'd come in, clean up, and go to sleep. He even started going to school on his own, preferring to catch a ride with one of his buddies or to walk with a group of friends, a group that didn't include me anymore.

I didn't know how to deal with the rejection, so for the most part, I ignored it. I overlooked his detachment and excused it by telling myself, *He's busy,* or *He's a popular guy, so everybody wants to be around him,* but inside I think it was the beginning of a change in me as well. I began to realize how much power Johnny had to hurt me, and slowly I pulled away in my own way.

Several months had passed without incident before we woke to the familiar sounds of our mother crying.

"Please, Stan," she wept, "don't kill me, baby. I love you."

It was early in the morning. Johnny was laying on his bed, his Walkman on his chest, having obviously fallen asleep the night before with his headphones on. Bo was fast asleep, a soft snore rising from his mouth. I stirred from sleep at what I thought was the TV. Confused and groggy, I laid on the floor, blinking slowly and straining to bring clarity to what I was hearing. Recognition hit me, and I lifted my head and peered at the door. My mother was crying. Instinctively I turned toward Johnny, but he'd heard nothing. I rose to my feet, panicked, ran to his bed, and shook him.

"Johnny," I whispered, glancing up toward the door.

"I'm sorry, baby," came the weeping again. "Please don't kill me."

"Johnny!" I said again, shaking him more urgently.

Johnny opened his eyes, sat up, and slid the headphones from his head. "What?" he said, annoyed.

"Mom's crying."

"She's always crying," he said.

"Listen!" I snapped, lifting my chin to the door again.

Again my mother's voice rang out softly in the morning. Johnny was right; it seemed as though she was always crying, but there was something different in her voice that morning, something urgent and desperate. Johnny listened closely, his eyes glued on the closed door, until he slowly shifted them and they fell on me. His mouth closed, and he swallowed hard. I copied him and swallowed too. He watched me, the wheels in his head turning, and it was then that I saw his face begin to change.

His eyes grew hard, his mouth drawn tight and thin, and he threw the sheet from his body and rose from the bed. "Come on," he said.

I stepped back, afraid to follow but even more afraid to stay, and drew close at his side as he approached the door and twisted the knob. The sound of hopelessness filled the hallway. My mother wept, her sobs spilling from her like water from the pipe. We stepped from the room tentatively. The air seemed humid and sticky, and the sounds of my mother crying created a sense of dread I had never, until that moment, experienced before.

Johnny walked with his fists balled at his side. His body was tense, and he stepped forward with purpose. I, on the other hand, lingered back. My hands were far from balled. I wrung them in front of me, breathing heavily as my tiny heart raced in my chest. I fought back tears and struggled to resist the urge to turn and lock myself in my room. But I couldn't *not* follow Johnny. It was like there was a cord tied from my waist to his, and with each step he took, somehow, miraculously, I took one as well. Johnny reached the corner of the hallway before I did, and I saw him draw to a sudden stop, his hands going limp at his side. His legs buckled beneath him, and he fought to remain standing.

I hurried forward, terrified to be standing alone, and came to the same sudden stop as I stood beside him. I felt Johnny's hand press against my chest, both to warn me back and keep me steady. We both stood and stared as the hallway opened into the living room, and we saw my mother standing in the middle of the room, her hands pressed together like a prayer, a shotgun hovering against her face.

Stirred by the movement, Mom shifted her eyes and saw us. I didn't know what I'd seen at the time, but it was that moment that I first recognized that she'd been damaged beyond repair. I saw brokenness in her eyes, a helpless acceptance that she was nothing more than a victim and that everything that happened to her was what she deserved. She shifted those painful eyes away from us and pressed them gently against my father once again.

"Please, Stan, don't kill me, baby."

I pulled my eyes away from her and saw a stranger holding the gun. His eyes were cold, unfeeling flames that bore into Mom and burned her flesh. His teeth were clenched shut, and I saw ripples along his cheek as he ground them down. There was no compassion in him. Those were not the eyes I knew when my father bounced me on his knee and threw me in the air. He was not the same man who would play his guitar and sing old Elvis Presley songs. Not the man who'd fill the room with music and twirl my mom around the living room, us children laughing while Mom pretended to resist him. That man was gone. He'd been drowned out by the black fire the drunken stranger loved to drink.

It wasn't all bad when I was growing up. There were times when I was so proud of my daddy, so much in love with him. I'd seen him do kind things for lots of people. I remember him helping my grandfather, lifting things that were too heavy or bringing him on a jobsite to supervise and paying him half of what they'd earned despite the fact that my dad had done all the work. There were times when we laughed, played, sang, and danced together. Times when I knew he was in love with my mom. Moments, when just by the way he looked at her, I could tell he cherished her. Occasions when he made me feel like the only person in the world.

But then there were those other times, moments that made me believe he was two people, moments like the one I'd walked into that morning. I couldn't accept that my father would hurt us the way he did, and so I created this other man, the drunken man, and blamed him for the painful times. Although I am grateful for those good times with Dad, in a way the inconsistency in him made everything hurt that much more. I remember being filled with hope when he sang to us, hope that maybe the pain was over, and the drunken man had left, only to have that hope stolen from me the next night with a punch or kick.

My relationship with him made it difficult for me to trust not only other people but myself. There are parts of me that wish he would have been one way or the other all the time. At least then I would have known what to expect from him. Each time he wasn't who I'd expected, it felt like betrayal, and the constant disappointments left me confused and resentful. If I'd have known that morning would be the last time I'd see my dad over the next twenty-two years, I might have tried to hold on to the good in him. As it was, I didn't, and all the good he'd ever done was erased in that single moment.

"Please, baby. Just put the gun down."

Mascara bled down my mother's face and encircled her eyes. Her lips quivered, and she gave a small cry, raising her hands slightly as my father lifted the gun farther. My heart pounded in my chest, and a terrified shout rose from my throat.

"Daddy, don't!"

I heard the gun blast ring out in the morning and shouted as my older brother placed a hand on my shoulder, turning to shelter me, and pressed us to the floor. I lay next to him, the sky raining down on us, and saw my mother standing, her hands covering her face, my father still holding the gun, standing motionless.

"You bastard!"

My mom shouted her fury, and then she was there beside us, helping us up from the floor, dusting us off and pulling us close, wrapping us in her strong embrace.

"I'm so sorry, baby," she cried, petting our faces, sliding our hair to the side. "Are you OK? I'm so sorry," she cried again. "I love you, babies. I love you so much."

As she held me, I saw my dad staring at the ceiling above us. I lifted my eyes and saw a massive hole peppered into the Sheetrock, small drafts of dust still floating in the air. I looked back in his direction and saw him lower the gun and turn toward us. Mom's hand rubbed my back, and my brother pressed firmly against my side as Dad walked by silently and disappeared down the hallway. I heard the back door slam shut, but I never looked toward the sound.

Mom stayed with us in the room for a long time before she finally rose from the floor and left. She quietly opened the door and closed it behind her, leaving us in silence. Sometime later, she returned, her face wild and afraid.

"Grab some clothes," she said, racing to the drawer in the corner. "Hurry!"

We rose and scurried around the room, grabbing clothes we wanted, confused and afraid.

"What's wrong, Mommy," I asked.

"Just get your stuff, Junior," she said. "We're leaving."

"Can I bring my toys?" I asked, concerned about leaving the things I cherished most.

"You can grab one," she managed to shout, still whispering.

I grabbed my *Thomas the Train* book, and Mom ushered us out the bedroom window. We fled from my father, fled for our lives, and stepped into a world full of different fears. It was the last time I'd see my dad as a child, but the fear we felt would continue to plague my family and me for a long time to come.

Five

MARCO POLO

There are wounds that never show on the body that are
deeper and more hurtful than anything that bleeds.

—LAURELL K. HAMILTON, *MISTRAL'S KISS*

It took a few weeks for my brother and me to believe we weren't
returning to my father. It wasn't the first time we'd fled, and every
other time, either he found us or Mom gave up and went back. That
morning we'd jumped into the car and driven back to Louisiana to stay
with an uncle. After a few days there, we drove back to Texas and hid
with my grandparents, and I don't remember what happened after that.
I know there were a series of different men in and out of our lives. Each
time Mom got a new boyfriend, we'd move in with them, but they never
seemed to last very long, so we ended up moving quite often.

When we left my father, I thought things would improve for us. I
knew that without him in the picture, we wouldn't have to worry about
him trying to kill my mom or hurt us. I truly thought things would be
better, but I was wrong. Things didn't get better. They got worse, and
before I knew it, I'd become a full-blown addict, and the drug of choice
was poverty.

I quickly learned that as confusing as life was with my dad, it was actually much simpler to deal with just him. At least we knew where the pain would come from. It was always the threat of violence. In a sense, it was more comfortable dealing with the beatings than the unknown this *new* life offered.

As young as I was, I'd already begun to understand the two rules my father had taught me. I was learning them and would have eventually been able to play his game. I'd seen the turning point in my brother, the change from identifying with our mother as a victim to embracing his aggression. But this new life, this brave new world my mother had brought us into, was a completely different game, with an entirely new set of rules, and I didn't understand it.

Not long after leaving Dad, my mom began to show the pregnancy she'd hidden from him, not wanting him to know of the daughter he'd fathered. My brothers and I soon had a sister, and not only did the size of our family change, but the way Mom treated us changed. She'd finally gotten her baby girl, and she doted on her with all her love and affection, leaving us behind.

Another change happened that greatly shaped who I am. I woke up one morning to find my older brother gone.

I stirred from sleep and left my room to wake Johnny, just as I'd always done. He was my safe place, my big brother, and the first thing I wanted to do every morning was see him. I turned the knob on his door (he had his own room now) and saw that he'd already woken from bed. I turned and went into the kitchen, but he wasn't there. I stumbled toward the bathroom to see if he was brushing his teeth, but he wasn't there either.

Groggy, I remained still, thinking about where he could be. "Mom!" I yelled.

"What?"

"I can't find Johnny." Silence. "Where is Johnny?" I asked.

I'll never forget her response. She barreled out of her bedroom, her face contorted with anguish and anger, and grabbed me by the hair, dragging me behind her as she pulled me back into my bedroom.

"What did I do?" I cried.

When we stepped through the door, she whirled me to the floor by my hair. "Don't mention his name again!" she yelled. "He's gone; that's all you need to know."

I huddled in a corner of the room as she left, slamming the door behind her. My world had been turned upside down. I was confused, uncertain, terrified because I was alone, and I didn't know how to be without him. I'd always followed my big brother's lead, and now he was gone, and I didn't know if I'd ever see him again. I never asked Mom about Johnny after that, and I adapted, as difficult as it was. I had no choice.

We moved frequently during that period, and I learned that nothing in life was permanent. We lived in rental homes with lots of bedrooms, always knowing that we wouldn't be there long, and never allowing ourselves to grow completely comfortable. We lived in apartment complexes, trailer parks, and government housing. One of the units we inhabited had no plumbing, and we were forced to shower at my grandparent's trailer once a week, on Sundays when we'd visit.

I loved those Sundays because my grandparents were always so loving and gentle toward us. Papa Cisco was strong and quiet, a prideful Mexican who'd worked his way from nothing into a steady job and a good marriage. And although some might have considered him poor, he was proud of his trailer because it was his, and he enjoyed life in spite of what little he had. I was proud of him too and admired his steadiness and unwavering integrity.

Granny was a big woman, and I loved to snuggle up in her arms and let her hold me as I curled into her lap. She smiled easily and had a thick French accent that made it hilarious to talk with her. Those were good times, filled with sweet thoughts of togetherness, but I have three memories from that time that I am most grateful for.

Every Sunday we would show up early (on the nights we didn't stay over), and there was always a big breakfast waiting for us. Oatmeal, bacon, eggs, toast, orange juice, and milk! There's still not a person I know who can make a bowl of oatmeal the way Granny did! She'd dump scoops of butter, pour spoonfuls of sugar, and then soak it with milk. Once she plunged her oversized spoon into the pot and stirred, we'd have a big, buttery, sugary soup. It was always a feast with them, and Papa Cisco required that we ate together, as a family, gathered around the table. There was laughter and sharing, smiles and a sense that the people there *really* loved us. That's memory one, breakfast around the table.

My second memory is about Papa Cisco. Before we could eat, he'd require that each of us bowed our heads, and he'd begin the most beautiful prayer I'd ever heard. I have no idea what he said (it was all in Spanish), but I always knew that he was praying for us. He was a serious man, and an earnest one, and when he prayed, it was filled with such intensity that I couldn't imagine a God who would not listen to him. Every time he finished with "Amen," I had the sense that my mess ups had just been accounted for.

My final memory is of our time in church. I was an emotional kid, erratic most of the time, transitioning from extreme happiness to violent outbursts continuously, but in church I always felt at peace. There was something about the belief that there was someone out there who loved me and who was in control of everything that made me feel better. In my mind this God fellow could beat up all the bad people, and even though they might hurt me now, in the end God would get revenge for me as long as I kept believing he would.

I also developed a sense of purpose in church, the belief that God allowed me to go through all the bad stuff so that he could use me for big things. I believed, I had to believe, that there was a reason for the pain. With a mother who convinced me I was evil, that I was going to hell, I needed to hold onto something that made me feel special, and at that time God was all there was.

Although Sundays were nice, the rest of my days were difficult, and the older I got, the more challenges I faced. We were still in the midst of living with different men my mom dated, and we were exposed to the more intimate side of male and female relationships during that time. It changed the way I saw my mother.

"Mom said we have to stay in the room," protested Bo.

"I don't care what she said," I fired back. "She's only saying that because that tow-truck driver is coming over."

Bo remained silent.

"I'm not going to let him hurt her," I declared. "You and me are going to go out there, but we'll have to be sneaky so they don't see us," I said. "We'll watch to make sure he doesn't do anything to her, and if he tries something, we'll jump out and start hitting him." I waited for Bo's confirmation. He nodded, and I warned him, "You better come with me when I go out there. It'll take both of us if he's big."

Bo nodded again.

That night, Roy showed up at the little house we stayed in behind The Rambling Rose, a bar my mom hung out at often, and Bo and I threw a blanket over us and made our move into the living room. We scooted on our bellies, making certain the blanket always concealed us, until we lay nestled deep into the left corner of the living room. We lifted the edge of the blanket so that we could peer out. All the lights were out, so it took a few moments for our eyes to adjust to the darkness, but then we saw them.

They were sitting on the couch kissing, my mom's hand tangled in his hair. Roy grabbed her side and helped as my mom lifted her top, her breasts spilling out, and then she stood to remove her pants. I shifted uncomfortably as my mother rose to her feet and began to remove his pants as well.

"He's about to hurt her," I whispered to my brother. "Get ready. I'll throw the blanket off, make a lot of noise, and jump on his back when he gets on top of her," I said, my eyes still glued to the scene in front of me. "You run up behind me and help."

We tensed as his pants fell to the floor. I dug my bare feet into the carpet and prepared to launch myself into the night and protect my mom. They kissed some more and touched one another, and then my mother pushed him back onto the couch and straddled him. My heart sank, and tears streamed from my eyes.

"Let's go," I whispered dejectedly. "He's not hurting her. She's the one who's doing it all."

We crawled back to the room and never spoke about it again. There's not much a seven-year-old can say to a six-year-old that would clear something like that up. I don't think it was the fact that my mom was having sex that bothered me as much as it was that *she* seemed so aggressive about it. After every failed relationship, she would complain and cry, telling us how much these men had hurt her, how they'd used her and threw her away like a piece of garbage. That night I realized that my mother was using them just as much as they were her, and it was a disappointment.

That night ended up being the start of another failed relationship, and six months later my brother and I were standing in a mechanic shop, helping my mom track down the man who'd never returned her calls.

Mom had gotten dressed up, her hair and makeup done, and she stood with my sister in her arms talking to a heavyset man in a gray shirt.

"Where is he?" I heard her ask.

"I don't know where he is," the man replied.

"You're lying to me!" she screamed. "I know that son of a bitch is here. You tell him…"

I stopped listening and turned to examine the machines that were all around. Bo and I wandered off, bored out of our minds, and got as far away from Mom's yelling and our sister's crying as we could.

"You want to play a game?" I asked, glancing around to see what we could do.

Bo nodded and smiled. "Marco Polo," he said.

"We're not in the pool," I shot back dismissively.

"We can close our eyes and walk around," he said.

I thought about it for a moment and then nodded. "OK. I'll go first. You yell 'Polo,' and I'll find you."

I closed my eyes excitedly and shouted out, "Marco!"

"Polo," replied my brother.

I could barely hear his voice, so I began walking with my hands pressed firmly out in front to prevent my running into anything. I shouted, and he shouted again. His voice was a little louder. I shouted; his reply grew still louder. I knew I was on the right track, and I began to walk faster. I called to him for a few more minutes until I heard him giggling at my efforts, and I knew I had to be close.

I shouted, "Marco!" and began to run forward.

"Polo," came the reply, directly in front of me.

I sprinted ahead and shouted one last time, "*Marc*—"

Lightning struck me between the eyes. I didn't know where I was or what had happened, but pain filled my head as it throbbed with white flashes of light. I vaguely heard my brother shouting, "Junior, are you OK?" and I felt hands grabbing me. I opened my eyes and realized I was on my back and there was a group of men surrounding me, talking all at once. I couldn't understand a word they were saying, and the confusion only frightened me further.

I screamed, "Get away from me!" I kicked at them and flailed my arms, "Stop it," I shouted. "Leave me alone!"

A set of strong hands gripped me by the shoulders and held me still with a firm grasp. "You hit your head, boy," he slurred, "and you're bleeding all over my damn floor."

It was then that I noticed the blood pouring from my face and into my mouth. The day would end with me in the emergency room and seven stitches in my forehead.

I tell this story not because it was traumatic for me—it wasn't—but because the physical hurt that we experienced, events like these, when we left my father, meant nothing. The emotional and psychological pain of seeing our mother move in and out of unhealthy relationships was far worse than anything else.

It was in this period in my life that the greatest changes occurred. With Johnny gone I was forced to stop being the quiet, insecure second son, and I was thrust into the role of what I thought the older brother should look like. Initially I saw myself as the defender, a cross between the toughness of my dad and the kindness of my brother, and I made the decision to protect those who couldn't protect themselves. That version of me didn't last long. It was rooted in a form of innocent idealism—and the more I experienced life, the faster that image deteriorated.

It's interesting the way my perspective changed once my father was no longer in the picture. As long as we all lived beneath the shield of his violence, there was a sort of shared misery that protected us from all the other dysfunction. I never noticed how cold my mom could be. I never paid attention or even considered that her decisions might be extremely self-serving, inconsiderate, or even hurtful. The thought of her being cruel or anything other than the damsel in distress never crossed my mind.

That all changed as she navigated through the murky waters of meaningless relationships and we sat on deck watching her compromise herself time after time. Don't get me wrong; I'm not saying, nor do I think, my mom is or was a bad person. Our life just became such that her shortcomings became undeniable and influential. In a way, my father's violence had sheltered us, as twisted as that might sound. It was so overwhelming, all-consuming, that any and every other deviation was rendered insignificant. With the absence of his violence, *every* dysfunction impacted us.

I remember the way my mom spoke: discussing sex, talking about people, cussing at my siblings and me with absolute indifference. Taking advantage of people who'd help us: money from churches, selling food stamps for cash, and so on. The lying, denying, and more than anything, the manipulation. It was as if I was suddenly thrust from a life of smothering fear into one of constant confusion, embarrassment, and disappointment.

I'm not still angry with my mother. I understand that she did the best she could with the experiences she was dealt. I won't go into the details of *her* story because it's not mine to tell, but if I'd have gone through what she went through, who knows? I may not have done as well as she did with us. I may have given the kids up altogether. It certainly would have made things easier. The fact that she kept our family intact says a lot about her strength and commitment.

Six

BULLDOG

This world I live in is empty and cold / the loneliness cuts me and tortures my soul.

—WAYLON JENNINGS

We moved more times than I can count. I remember feeling so proud of a rental home we were able to stay in. It had four bedrooms and a swimming pool in the backyard, and I couldn't wait for my friends to see it. We weren't there long enough for me to show it off. Shortly after, I'm not sure how much later, we moved out and into one of several different apartments, and it was that time in our lives that I started choosing the wrong path. I can't say that I started going down the wrong path, because I was born on the wrong side to begin with, but it was the first time that I began making decisions that weren't good for me, of my own accord.

Third grade was a turning point. I was a skinny kid, malnourished, with long, stringy hair, and scared of my shadow. I remember the fear, this constant weight I carried, but what made it difficult was the fact that there was always a burning desire to be brave. I longed to be tough enough, mean enough, scary enough for people to accept me, and every time I let fear win, I was overcome with shame.

I always looked for ways to fit in. I remember when rolling your pants up at the ankles was in style, and the only pants I had that fit me the way I liked were brown bell-bottoms, and so I would roll them up tight and walk around as confidently as I could. I'd clean my shoes constantly or try to get haircuts that were popular, but it seemed like I always had the *For Dummies* version of everything.

Unfortunately, the pants weren't enough to turn me into one of the cool kids, and I still got pushed around by a couple of bullies. I was walking home from school late one day when I saw my opportunity, and I took it. The two kids who were always picking on me were chasing down another boy, much larger than I was, and he was surprisingly fast. He was cutting across the field in between the school and our apartments, and he was so far out in front of them that I knew they'd never catch him.

I've always been fast, so I dropped my books and sprinted across the field after this other boy, running scared for his life. I tackled him, throwing him down to the ground, and pushed my knee into his chest to hold him down. Exhilarated, I turned my head and saw the two pursuers shouting and cheering as they ran up fast. I knew what this boy had coming to him; they'd beaten me a couple of times in a similar way.

I couldn't understand it at the time, but I am grateful for it now. I looked down at this kid as he shouted out, "Please let me go!" and I knew I didn't want to be a villain. I didn't want to be the reason he got beaten in the same way I'd been beaten, and so I fell forward on him and whispered, "I'm going to let you go. *Run!*" The boy pushed up, and I fell over as he rose to his feet and ran.

The two boys, we'll call them Peter and Robby, arrived a few seconds later, expressing their disappointment.

"Damn it," yelled Peter, slapping his hands against his legs. "You had him."

"I tried to hold him," I said, "but he's a big dude."

Robby watched as the chubby kid kept running until he reached the main street, and then he shifted his eyes to me. "I didn't know you were that fast."

I stared up, not saying anything.

"What's your name?" asked Peter.

"I'm Junior," I told them, standing and dusting the grass from my tightly rolled bell-bottoms.

From that day on, I was one of the cool kids. I went everywhere with Robby and Peter, even got a girlfriend who lived in their town houses, and got to hang out with them and their families. Robby's family was strict, and his dad was hard on him, but I loved staying at Peter's. He got anything he wanted, any time, and his mother treated him as if he was her reason for living. She'd buy hamburgers and pizza for us, and by the time we were in the fourth grade, she was letting Peter drive her car.

They became my friends in school too, and that's when I started getting into trouble. I never felt good enough when I was around them, but I felt worthless without them, so I did everything I could to prove to them that I belonged. I started fighting a lot, cussing at teachers, and even pulled a junior-level drug heist with cinnamon oil and typing paper that landed me with a three-day suspension and half a day of returning money to the kids I'd sold to. Each step along the way, Peter and Robby were there to cheer me on. I grew progressively worse until other kids noticed me, and before I knew it, I was the cool kid, or at least the notorious one, and I ditched Peter and Robby and started running with kids who were into *real* trouble.

I began hanging out in Park Hollow apartments, and it was there that I met Owen, the biggest drug dealer in town. I befriended him quickly and soon was hanging out in the apartments until two, sometimes three, in the morning, smoking weed and drinking. My mom was clueless about what was going on with me. In her defense, her life was still full of trouble and uncertainty. She'd finally met a guy who seemed to genuinely love her, and that meant stability for us. But for my mom, she struggled with allowing him to love her, often times causing fights or drama in an effort to drive him away.

I understand the challenge my mom faced emotionally, now that I'm an adult. I have the same struggle, even now. It's amazing at how deeply dysfunction can imbed itself into our psyches. I'm thirty-eight years old and a highly successful man, and I still struggle with the thought that I'm not good enough, that somehow I am unlovable. There are times when I feel the compulsion to act out in my relationships, to push on those who love me, just to see if they love me enough to stay, even when I'm not perfect. I've gotten better at managing the urges, but I've accepted that this constraint is one that will never go away.

It was Owen who first introduced me to drugs. He gave me my first joint and had me selling for him within the first week. I was what they called a *mule*, carrying the product to different apartments, where I would trade it for cash. Once I finished the transactions, I'd then bring the money back to Owen, where he'd pay me with cash and drugs. I couldn't believe my luck. Owen was the toughest man around, and he chose me to work for him. I felt so fortunate and as if overnight I'd discovered what I wanted to be; I wanted to be just like Owen.

Although I was in the third grade, I always felt invincible. I thought I could fight off any threat, and if I couldn't, I knew Owen would protect me. I never considered that there might be a time when Owen wasn't there and I wasn't big enough to fight off the threat.

My friend Steven and I were making our rounds in the complex when we came upon a guy everyone called "Bulldog." He was a stocky man, very muscular, bald, with tattoos on his face.

"What's up?" he said as we walked by.

I nodded and replied, "What's up?"

He was leaning against the wall beside the door to an apartment. "Y'all putting in work?" he asked.

Steven answered, "Yeah, just running some stuff for Owen."

I looked at him crossways and continued walking. I didn't like when people asked questions, and I didn't like that Steven so easily volunteered answers.

"Wait a minute!" yelled Bulldog. "Why don't y'all take a break and chill with me?"

"Naw, we're good, dog. We gotta get this stuff gone," I said.

"I know that, but you can take a break. Smoke some weed with me," he said, throwing his arms out, as if to say, "Come on."

Steven looked at me and pleaded. "Come on, Junior. We can stop to smoke something, man. Owen won't care, as long as we get everything sold."

I knew something was wrong, but I was too insecure to argue at the time. Steven was asking me to stay, and there was Bulldog, watching us intensely. "All right, fine," I said. "We'll smoke something with you."

We all entered his apartment. It was completely empty aside from a blanket and a pillow on the floor. There were holes in the wall and stains on the carpet, but other than that, the apartment was empty.

"Go on and sit down," said Bulldog, pointing at the floor.

We sat down while he walked over to the kitchen to grab a bag off the bar. He came back with a sack of weed and took a seat across from us.

"Y'all ever smoke this purple lights shit?" he asked.

"No," I replied, leaning forward to get a better look.

"Here," he said, handing me a wad of bud. "You feel how sticky that shit is?"

"Yeah," replied Steven, taking it from my hand. "I bet this smokes good."

"You don't even know," replied Bulldog, placing some bud in a zag and rolling it up. He lit the joint, hit it hard, and held his breath until at last the sweet smell of northern lights filled the room. He passed it to me.

I hit it as hard as he did. That was a mistake. The next thing I remember is feeling like I was on a train, traveling a hundred miles per hour, backward through the wall. I passed the joint to Steven and looked up to see Bulldog staring at me, a knowing smile on his face.

"It's good, isn't it?" he asked.

"Man, I'm so blowed," I replied.

I don't remember the entire conversation, but I know at some point I began to grow uncomfortable. Steven was completely lost. He'd continued to smoke, but I'd stopped when I realized how strong it was. I never lost sight of the fact that I had a lot of dope and a lot of cash on me. That's why I noticed when Bulldog stood, went to the door, and locked it.

"What are you doing, dog?" I asked, alarmed.

"I can't have nobody walking in here while we're getting high," he replied. "Just a precaution."

I looked at Steven, who was giggling to himself, his eyes rolling back into his head, and realized that he was completely useless. Bulldog walked back to where he had been sitting and continued talking.

"Yeah, I just did a dime on some home-invasion shit. You ever been locked up?" he asked.

"No," I said.

"It ain't as bad as everyone makes it out to be. You find your way while you're in there." He took another hit and grinned. "I got a lot of ass while I was in there."

My heart sank. He took another hit and stared at me, the grin gone, replaced with a serious, contemplative look.

"I got a *lot* of ass in there," he said again. "You ever get you some ass, boy?"

"No," I said again.

"You ever give that ass up?" he asked.

"No." I swallowed hard.

"No," he repeated, "not even once? You've got to at least try it once," he said, rising to his feet. "You might like it." He began walking toward the bar again and ordered over his shoulder, "Take off your clothes."

He turned his back, reaching over the bar for something, and I shook Steven urgently. "Come on, man; we gotta go."

"Why, dude? This is good stuff," he replied, halfway out of it.

"We gotta go, man. He wants to rape us," I said, rising to my feet and moving toward the door.

"Where y'all going?" shouted Bulldog from the kitchen. "The fun is just starting." He stepped around the bar, moving toward us.

I twisted the doorknob, but it was locked. I pulled at it, tried unlocking it, but for some reason I couldn't get it to open. Bulldog was moving fast now, right at me.

"This way, Junior," said Steven, sliding the front window open and leaping out.

I hurriedly moved from the door to the window, and just as I jumped over, I felt Bulldog grab at my shirt. I chopped down with my hand, breaking his grip. He leaned out the window and smiled.

"Come on, man; we're just having fun, that's all. You smoked my weed and now you're just going to leave?"

Steven and I turned and ran without looking back to see if he was following us. We sold the rest of the dope that was on us and brought the money back to Owen. He paid us, and though I thought about telling him what happened, in the end I only kept my mouth shut. I was embarrassed and afraid of making an enemy out of Bulldog. For the next year and a half, I avoided him as often as I could and never let myself be alone when he was around. That day I learned that I was much, much more vulnerable than I'd realized.

Seven

POVERTY

We all have a Monster within; the
difference is in degree, not in kind.

—DOUGLAS PRESTON, *THE MONSTER OF FLORENCE*

When I think about these experiences, it's so hard to believe I survived. I was playing around in a world of gangsters and killers, and I had no idea, yet so much of who I am was shaped during that time of my life. This is when I learned about poverty and what it truly looks like.

Most people think of money when they hear the term "poverty," but not having money means you're poor, and being poor is different than being impoverished. Colin Powell recently talked about poverty as a mind-set, and to some degree he is right. True poverty takes place in the mind first and then acts out in the world, behaviorally, within the context of relationships second.

The people I saw as different from or better than me were people who lived with ethically or morally based value systems. They were the people who did an honest day's work, who helped others in need, and who were always friendly and fun to be around. Most of the people I knew like this were from school. Teachers, my principals, and even some of the *good kids* seemed to live by this other set of rules. I never wanted to be like them because I thought they were too different, like another species, and it doesn't make sense for a dog to want to be a cat. I was a dog in a dog-eat-dog world. Who'd want to be a cat anyway?

In poverty we functioned with a survival-based value system, which was a perversion of the former. Whereas in a morally based value system, people value relationships above all else, in poverty we valued possessions. Even our relationships were viewed as possessions. Every decision we made was centered around what we could attain, regardless of the cost. A great example was the big-screen TV we had in our trailer, yet there was no food in the refrigerator. Here, a mother values the television over providing for her dependent children. Or when I was out at the club with my guys, we were willing to take a guy's life so that we could have his shoes. In our eyes, those tennis shoes were more valuable than another man's life.

It's the same with drugs. They are a means to possessions, and the number of lives it costs to get those possessions is irrelevant. Carjackings, robberies, home invasions—all have the same end in mind. This is what poverty is, and the reason we, as a society, have been losing the fight is because we have misidentified the enemy. I know poor people who are morally and ethically sound. Single mothers who raise their children to be upstanding citizens with bright futures. Though they are poor, they are not impoverished.

On the other hand, I know very wealthy people who develop drug addictions, become alcoholics, abandon their families for work, and so on. Although they have massive amounts of money, they live in poverty. All money does is change the face of poverty, but it doesn't eliminate it. Once society is able to grasp this concept, only then will we be able to make progress in this war on poverty. The key is to abandon the notion that money is the answer and start focusing on how people do relationships. It may sound hokey, but the implications for repairing relationships, particularly in impoverished homes, is astounding. All the data indicates that relational connectedness is the key to eliminating every factor that puts people at risk. I know the data is spot on because I *am* the data.

We all know that education is the key to success in today's world. It may be through college, or it may be through trade schools or some other avenue. Regardless of where an education is gotten, education itself is essential. So let's look at what poverty is costing us in schools.

Most teachers function with a morally/ethically based value system; at least if they're healthy adults, they do. If the survival-based value system of poverty is a perversion of a teacher's value system, then naturally there is going to be some conflict when the two systems collide in the classroom. As a result of this conflict, more times than not, a disconnectedness develops between the teacher and the student, making it impossible to establish anything but an oppositional relationship. The student makes the teacher's life a living hell, and the teacher either quits his or her job (some leave education altogether) or gets rid of the student.

So now the student is at home, the only healthy, appropriate adult in his or her life has rejected him or her, something he or she interprets as "See? You're not good enough for them," and so he or she looks to the other adults in his or her life to get approval. Adults who themselves are perpetrators of poverty. The student then either returns to school worse than he or she was before he or she left or never returns to school and fully embraces poverty without teachers to act as a buffer against it. The person has children and raises his or her children in poverty (survival-based value system), and then those children go to the same school and have the same teacher who kicked their mother or father out of school. Do you see what I mean? It becomes an ugly cycle that feeds itself, making everyone within it miserable.

The alternative, recognizing that there is a clash in value systems and approaching it with intentionality, can lead to deep, meaningful relationships for students. These types of connections can mean the difference between success and failure or even, in some cases, life or death. It can mean that teachers are finally respected and valued for the incredible service they offer this country, and perhaps it would mean that they are reminded of the greater purpose they serve.

What I needed more than anything was for an appropriate adult, someone who'd navigated the choppy waters of adolescence and who had managed to enter into adulthood with his or her honor intact, to simply show me the way. I didn't know how to be anything other than what I was, and *that* is the great advantage poverty has. Oftentimes I hear people say, "It was just normal for me," or "I didn't see anything wrong; it was just life," and they are absolutely telling the truth. Poverty so distorts reality that the distortion itself becomes reality, and everything else is a dream not worth having because it's just that, a dream. Something unattainable.

The only way to dig oneself out of the twistedness of poverty is to have a guide, so to speak, someone to be an anchor point as those in poverty try to pull themselves up out of the bottomless well they're stuck in. It's a difficult process, perhaps the most difficult thing I've ever had to overcome, and it's a lifelong process. I'm nearing forty, and the survival-based system still attempts to creep into my thoughts on occasion. My saving grace has been the appropriate adults in my life and their endless love and support, even in the midst of mistakes.

I do want to clarify what I mean by *love* as well. True love isn't simply being nice or accepting or concerned with making a person feel good. I'm an aggressive guy with violent tendencies. If someone were to allow me to act inappropriately and simply tried to *love* my behavior away by being accepting, supportive, and encouraging, I would walk all over them and continue my inappropriate behavior. I would guess that most people in poverty would do the same. The problem with this kind of love is that it's perceived as weakness or disingenuous. In a survival-based value system, people don't simply accept pain unless they are a victim (and worthy of spite or disrespect) or setting a person up for something.

Real love requires that we accept the person while condemning the behavior. It requires courage and strength enough to call a person out and hold him or her accountable when he or she behaves inappropriately.

It's important to do so out of disappointment, which communicates that you expect more, rather than doing so out of anger. All anger does is confirm that you're like every other adult in their lives and therefore you deserve the same kind of respect as every other adult in their lives.

By loving a person in poverty—holding them accountable, expecting higher-level behavior, accepting the person while condemning the behavior, and communicating genuine caring—you are able to establish the fact that you're not like the other people in their lives and that you deserve a higher level of respect than they're accustomed to giving. In this way, you motivate someone in poverty to question their beliefs because of their desire to live up to the expectations the appropriate adult has for them.

What's key during this process is consistency. You have to go into this process knowing that the poverty-based person will fail. When they fail it is an opportunity to challenge their behaviors using the love I spoke about earlier. If done in a consistent way, more times than not, the relationship with the student or whomever it is deepens significantly, only strengthening that person's desire to do better and be better. The message that person receives is "I'm not like every other adult in your life. I'm not going away, even when you disappoint me. You can count on me to be here."

One of the challenges from poverty that I still carry with me is a sense of abandonment. I learned early in life that people were untrustworthy and that they left you when they were tired of you or when you lost in competition. In response I grew violent and sabotaged any and every relationship in my life out of fear of it ending eventually anyway. If I was able to end it, at least then I didn't have to worry about when it would happen, and I didn't have to suffer being abandoned. The problem with that is that what I desired more than anything was a deep, meaningful relationship, even though my behaviors communicated the absolute opposite message.

Ruby Payne has done some great work on poverty, and the most important aspect of her writing is that of communication. In poverty, when kids say, "I hate you," what they're saying is "You couldn't possibly love me." When their behaviors say, "Get as far away from me as possible," what they're saying is, "I desire a relationship with you, but I'm terrified you'll hurt me too." Every message comes down to those two statements. Poverty, at its core, has two rules: there are victims and perpetrators, and we're not built for relationships because people can't possibly love you.

By demonstrating that life is more than victims and perpetrators, that it's filled with allies and collaborators as well, and by *loving* people consistently through successes and failures, you launch an attack against the very heart of poverty. Every other effort to fight poverty is a misplaced effort inevitably destined to fail.

Eight

FROM BAD TO WORSE

My life is a perfect graveyard of buried hopes.

—L. M. MONTGOMERY, *ANNE OF GREEN GABLES*

By the time I was in middle school, things had gotten worse for my family. My older brother was gone, my mom was single for some time, and we were living in a motel room off Spencer Highway in Pasadena. I'd have never believed it if you would have told me life would get worse without my father in the picture, but it did. I felt so ashamed of my family, and of myself, and I hid that shame behind anger and violence.

I was a troubled kid, and I brought trouble with me wherever I went. By the time I was in seventh grade, I'd already been expelled from school on a couple of occasions, been taken to the juvenile detention center more than once, and faced possible charges being filed against me for assault and battery. I did everything I could to keep people at a distance, and one of the lessons I'd learned is that the more violent you were, the further away people stayed.

We fell on very hard times, and at one point we found ourselves without a place to stay. We headed to Louisiana to stay with my mom's father again. I know that was a difficult decision for my mom, and if there would have been any other alternative, I believe she would have taken it. As it happened, there were no other choices, and so we ended up with an uncle who was completely inappropriate, and at twelve years old, I was sexually assaulted.

I can remember him on top of me, talking to me, my face pressed down into a pillow. There is no need to go into details here. My mother walked in on what was happening, and she furiously grabbed me and pulled me from the bed. My uncle had rolled off and tried to pretend he'd been asleep. I began crying as she dragged me into the living room by my arm and threw me onto the couch. She told me to keep my mouth shut because those types of things didn't happen in our family, before going off to bed.

I cried myself to sleep that night. I remember wondering why that had happened to me. What had I done to deserve such a brutal and violent attack? Why didn't my father want us? Why didn't my mother love us? Why didn't she protect me? Why hadn't she held me and told me that everything was going to be all right? At twelve years old, I was completely alone, absolutely enwrapped in shame and disappointment, and just plain tired.

The next morning, I woke up, and breakfast was ready at the table. *He* was sitting at the table along with everyone else, and I had to take my seat across from him. We all ate our food quietly. I never looked up from my plate, and no one else ever said anything. My mom never said anything.

I don't blame my mother for how she responded to what was happening. Without going too much into *her* story, she had been abused time and time again when she was a child, and I think the reality that the same thing had happened to one of her children was too much for her to handle. She'd made a vow to protect her children from the types of experiences she'd had as a child, and her failure was overwhelming. I don't blame her, but the pain was real nonetheless.

We left that house that morning and never went back. The drive to Texas was a long one. I was in pain physically and emotionally. My brothers fought with one another, fights I was usually in the middle of, but I just didn't have it in me. So many thoughts rushed through my head, all thoughts about how disgusting and shameful I was. I felt like garbage, believed I was garbage, and I hated myself.

There are so many children in the world today who are abused and taken advantage of in every way imaginable. I work in schools that don't have time to worry about what kind of grades their kids are making because they are too busy visiting with the FBI about child sex trafficking, kids who are being sold by their own parents. Children who are being forced to drink and try drugs as early as 5 years old. Children who are sexually active, having children at ten, eleven, twelve years old.

A couple of weeks had passed since I'd been assaulted by my uncle, and things only continued to get worse for me. I fell deeply into depression and lost interest in everything. I fell so low that there came a point when I just couldn't deal with life any more. I sat on my shower floor in the bathroom, the door locked, steam fogging the mirror, slicing my wrist. I watched blood swirl down the drain, waiting to die, wanting to die. My younger brother saved my life that day.

There was a banging at the door. I did not answer.

"Junior," cried Bo, "are you OK?"

I said nothing.

"Are you OK, Junior?" he asked again.

Still no answer.

My brother's voice grew panicked now. "Junior, come out of there; I'm scared. Just come out."

I sat on the floor and listened to his words, tears being washed away by the steaming water flowing from the shower spout. His words reminded me that he needed me. I realized that if I died there would be no one there to protect him. No one there to take the brunt of the blows that would inevitably come at him throughout the rest of his life. He needed me to live, and suddenly I wanted to live.

"I'm OK, Bo," I replied. "I'll be out."

I patched up my wrist, and that day I lived for my brother. In that moment I also made a decision. My father's life rules came back to me—*either you hurt people or they hurt you*—and I decided right there that I wasn't going to allow people to hurt me again. I decided that I would become the aggressor, and I'd soon have an opportunity to prove it.

My mom, in the meantime, began dating someone else, and we moved into a house with him. He seemed like a good man, willing to take on a woman with four children. He was a baker at a donut shop and worked extremely hard, having long nights and sleeping during the day. I adjusted to him fairly quickly, keeping my distance and weary of a relationship with him, but he didn't seem to mind. He actually took an interest in us kids and attempted to create more normal situations for us: playing catch, taking us camping, bringing us to work with him on the weekends so that we could eat donuts all night long.

Things would go terribly wrong with this man and forever change my life. It started with a phone call from school after I'd gotten into trouble for defending myself against a girl. She outweighed me by about fifty pounds and had started punching me in the head because I'd turned her down. I jumped up from the table and started swinging back, only to have one of the teachers pretty much tackle me to the floor. I was taken to the office, where the principal, a man who did not like me at all, called home.

The phone rang. "Hello, Mrs. Griffin."

"Yeah," replied my mother.

"I've got Junior in the office here. You'll need to come and remove him from the premises. He's being expelled from school for fighting with a girl in the cafeteria during lunch."

I'm not sure what my mom said on the other line, but the principal told me they said they would take care of me when I get home. I was furious I was the one in trouble. I had no intention of hitting a girl, but she would have beaten me up in front of the entire school if I hadn't rose to defend myself. The principal hung the phone up and began yelling at me. I bit my tongue for as long as I could, but there hit a point when I just couldn't contain myself anymore.

"Forget you!" I screamed out. "I don't give a damn about this school."

"What did you say?" replied the principal, a large man, rising from his chair and leaning over the desk.

I stood from my chair as well. "You heard me. I said forget you and this school. I don't give a shit about being here." I balled my fists, waiting for him to come around from the other side of his desk.

He glared at me, his own fists clenched and pressed into the desk-top. "Get the hell out of my school" is all he said, pointing toward the double glass doors.

I grabbed my chair and threw it, knocking it to the floor, and then turned and left the school building. Before heading home, I swung by the apartment building behind the school to catch up with a friend (who was much older than me). I'd brought several hundred dollars to school with me with the intention of buying a small .380-caliber gun. It didn't take long to find him, standing out near his car, the stereo speakers thumping in the parking lot, and we made the exchange and I had my gun.

I cried on the way home. I couldn't understand why I couldn't stay out of trouble. There were days I'd wake up and ask myself, *How can I avoid getting into trouble today?* and have no answer. It felt like bad things just happened to me, whether I wanted them to or not. I was so hopeless because I didn't want to be a bad kid. I wanted people to like me, not to be afraid of me. I just didn't know how to make that happen. When I was nice to people, they were disinterested in me. When I was ruthless, fighting, causing trouble, or cracking jokes, people paid attention, and I wanted to be noticed more than anything.

When I got home, my mom and her boyfriend were waiting for me outside. She was crying, and he had a belt in his hands.

"You screwed up again," said my mom, her arms folded across her chest.

Stanley Leone Jr.

"Come here," demanded her boyfriend, the belt hanging slack in his hands.

I don't know how to explain what happened to me in that moment, but I felt rage overtake me, and the next thing I knew, I was pointing the gun at this man who wanted to hurt me.

"Put your hands on me," I challenged. "Go on and hurt me now," I pressed on, pushing the gun toward him.

He took a step back, and my mother stepped in front of him so that the gun was aimed on her. Her hands came up, and she began rubbing them together, very subtlety rocking from side to side. Mascara began bleeding down her cheeks.

"Please don't hurt me, Junior. I love you, baby. Please don't hurt me," cried my mom.

I stood there, holding the gun out in front of me, so terribly angry, when I suddenly had what can only be called a flashback. I was 5 years old again, watching my father hold a gun in my mother's face, and I realized in that moment that I had become my father. I hated him, but all the anger, the hatred, and the violence did nothing to make me different from him. In fact, it was those things that made me just like him. When I realized that, I couldn't hold my hand up. I felt defeated, and I dropped my arm and held the gun at my side. The moment I did, a cop car, sirens blasting, pulled up in front of our house.

I dropped the gun on the ground, turned, and stood near the road in the driveway. The cop stepped from his car, gun in hand, and asked where the weapon that I'd had was. I pointed at the gun, now laying in the dirt driveway, and he made his way toward it. Picking it up he walked back to his car and set it in the front seat before turning and heading back toward me. He placed me in handcuffs and began walking me toward the car when he stopped and stepped in front of me.

"You've got two options here, boy," he said, surprisingly gentle. "I can take you down to the detention center," he said, "or you can get some help for yourself." He placed a hand on my shoulder. "You need some help, don't you?"

Tears fell down my cheeks. It was the first time I'd publicly cried in my life, and I could only nod. The officer noticed the bandage on my right wrist where I'd patched up the cuts. He realized I was a hurt kid, not a violent criminal, and because he gave me an alternative, I was taken downtown Houston to the second ward and locked in HCPC, the psych ward.

Nine

I Ain't Crazy; I'm Bipolar

*Some are born mad, some achieve madness, and
some have madness thrust upon 'em.*

—Emile Autumn, *The Asylum for Wayward Victorian Girls*

I spent most of my time in the psych center sitting around feeling
sorry for myself. There was a lot of time to think, and the more I
thought, the more I hated myself and despised my family. I couldn't
figure out why my father didn't want me and my mother didn't love me.
I was still so hurt from when my uncle raped me, and smaller things,
like other kids making fun of me, felt bigger than life. At that point in
my life, the only way out I could see was to end it all, to be done with
everything.

There were a lot of kids locked up with me, and just about all of
them were crazy. Julio, a small-statured Hispanic kid with dark hair and
dark eyes, heard voices but could draw anything he saw. Chuck was a
large boy, over six feet tall and built like the train that had hit him, taking half of his face—and his mind. He walked around all day repeating,
"The little wouldn't do, so the little got mo and mo, whoa." There was
Joey, a tall, lanky boy with short blond hair, who had a way of making

me feel even more uncomfortable than I already was. The first day I was there, he forced me to fight him.

I'd walked into the men's bathroom we all shared, where Joey and Ruben, his lackey, were waiting.

"We're gonna fight," said Joey. "Put these on." He handed me a pair of socks.

"What?" I asked.

"You're going to fight," repeated Ruben.

I grew scared and laid the socks down on the sink. "I don't want to fight," I said. Joey was much bigger than me, with long, lanky arms and a big jaw.

"You're going to fight, or I'm just going to whip your ass," declared Joey, pulling the socks over his hands.

"He's going to whip your ass whether you put the socks on or not," said Ruben.

Joey was nearly finished pulling the socks onto his hands, and so I picked up my pair and pulled them on, one hand at a time. I squared up with Joey and waited for them to sound the start, when suddenly he punched me in the jaw. I saw stars and raged. I don't remember exactly what happened, but somehow I'd been able to start swinging, furiously, and before I knew it, Joey was yelling out.

"OK, OK! That's it!"

I stopped swinging, my heart racing, and saw that Joey's nose was bleeding. He smiled, blood running into his teeth.

"Good job," he said, pulling off his socks. "Welcome to the center."

The best thing I could have done was defend myself because after that neither Joey nor Ruben harassed me again. There were other people in the center, all with their own issues, and each one I met only proved that I was indeed crazy. They confirmed that something was wrong with me, a belief I'd always had anyway.

There was Jaimie, a nymphomaniac who was willing to fool around with any of us guys (except for Chuck), and Jared, a full-blown drug addict. There was Freddy, a hyperactive compulsive liar, who walked around making up stories about things he'd done on the outside. And there was the kid who stayed in the padded room every day, all day, talking to Satan. Then there was me, the boy who'd been raped and abandoned by his family, the boy who'd tried to kill himself. I fit right in.

By the time I was in there for a couple of weeks, I'd gotten used to the way things were done. There was an unspoken routine and hierarchy, and as long as I played by the rules, things went along smoothly. The more comfortable I grew, the louder I got, and before long I was cussing as loudly as I could, complaining about everything. My favorite word was the *F*-word, and I shouted it out as often as possible.

I was complaining about the powdered eggs one morning, my head down, pushing my fork through the glop of food, when suddenly I heard a booming voice.

"What's your problem, boy!"

I was a bad seventh-grade kid, and if anyone asked me what my problem was, *like that*, I was going to let you know. In fact, my entire goal would be to give you a couple of problems of your own. I jumped up from my seat, my fists balled, ready to fight the man who'd just called me out. Now let me remind you that I was in the seventh grade. I came from a poor family, and so I was skinny enough to see the bones in my chest, and no taller than 5'2". When I looked up, I realized I was staring at this man's kneecaps.

He had to be somewhere around 6'5", 330 pounds. He, by far, was the largest man I'd ever seen. I glared at him, and although he was much bigger, I was much crazier. I'd always been a fighter, and I learned that the bigger a person was, the more of a reputation you got for knocking them out. I threw my chest out and readied myself. He stood straight, cutting his eyes down at me, and without explanation I sat down as quickly as I could and began to cry.

It was the second time in my life I'd ever cried in public. I didn't understand what was happening at the time, but now I realize that I was at a point in my life when I just needed to talk about the heartache and pain I'd felt. I couldn't hold it in anymore because I was so tired from carrying it around with me for all those years. I began to tell that man about all the things that had happened to me, all the things I was told you keep your mouth shut about.

Before I knew it, stories about my father, my mother, my uncle, other kids who laughed at me in school, the fear of walking through apartments at night, and carrying drugs from one unit to the other began spilling out. I told him about how much I hated myself. I admitted that every time I looked in the mirror I saw garbage, someone who wasn't good enough. Someone who was unlovable. When I finished I didn't know what to do because he was an adult, which meant he was the enemy. It had been the adults in my life who'd hurt me, not other kids. So if you were an adult, you were the enemy; you were guilty by association, and I'd just made myself completely vulnerable to the enemy.

I rose from my seat, the big man still silent, and began walking away from the table toward my room. I was about halfway away when I heard him shout.

"Come here, boy!"

Without thinking I turned and headed back toward the table.

"Sit down," he commanded.

I sat down as quickly as I could. I was terrified. I didn't know what to expect, but instead of hurting me, he opened up and began to share his own story with me. I was shocked and amazed. He told me about his mother, who turned tricks out of their one-bedroom apartment to put food on the table. He told me about his incarcerated father.

"You think you're the only one who's angry with your dad, boy?" he asked. "You don't think I ain't angry that my father chose being a gangsta over being a daddy? The only communication I have with my father is when my pencil meets the paper. You don't think I ain't angry?"

He told me about being a black man growing up in Houston in the fifties.

"You think you're the only one who feels like you're not good enough, kid? I know all about it. I couldn't drink out of your water faucet. I couldn't use your bathroom or walk on your side of the street.

I couldn't walk into a building the same way you walk into a building. You think you're the only one that feels like you're not good enough?" He paused and took a breath. My heart pounded. "I know all about it, kid."

When he finished his story, I didn't know what to do with it because he was still the enemy; he was just an enemy with his own set of issues. So I rose from my seat, thanked him for sharing, and turned to walk back to my room. At about halfway there, I heard him shout out again.

"Come here, boy."

I returned to the table and took my seat. He continued to share with me; telling me about education and how getting one changed his life.

"If you want the world to get big, you've got to get smart. The smarter you get, the bigger the world is."

He told me about graduating high school and enrolling in college, and he realized that the world was bigger than Houston. He told me about graduating college and how he realized then that the world was bigger than his state. He began traveling, seeing miraculous sights across the globe, and he realized that the world wasn't just bigger than America; it was just big, period.

"The smarter you get, the bigger the world becomes."

When he was finished, I thanked him for sharing with me and stood to leave once again.

"Come here, boy," he said once again, stepping closer to me from around the table.

I bowed up and tensed, terrified at his proximity to me. Closer, he stepped closer, until at last he hovered over me, and I prepared for the worst. I felt so vulnerable. I was vulnerable. He could have hurt me in any way he wanted, and there wouldn't have been a thing I could have done about it. I braced as he leaned down, and before I knew it, I was wrapped in a full embrace, my feet dangling off the ground. He'd leaned down and hugged me, lifting me into the air. I was terrified. Both of my arms were trapped at my sides, and I knew for certain he was going to hurt me—when his face fell into my shoulder and he began weeping.

I was stunned, trying to process what was happening. *Let's see: he's holding me up so he can cry on my shoulder?* How does something like that work? I didn't know what to do, so I did the only thing I could think of. I managed to get one hand free, and I took it and patted him on the back with it.

"It's OK," I told him. "I understand now."

When he finished crying, he dropped me to the ground and then walked away from me forever. I never got the opportunity—rather, I never took the opportunity—to tell him how much I appreciated his willingness to open up and share with me. I never thanked him, but nonetheless that ended up being a hug that changed my life. I learned that he was a counselor in the psychiatric center, named Joe, and he did two things for me in that single conversation, a conversation that lasted no more than ten minutes.

First, I realized that pain and suffering wasn't unique to me. I realized that other people got hurt too, and there was something so liberating about that realization. When you think you're alone, that you're the only one who goes through difficult times, it overwhelms you with shame and grief. I felt dirty and unlovable because I thought I was the only one who was abused in the ways I'd been abused. His willingness to share about his own pain made it not quite so bad for me.

Secondly, I realized there was a way out. He'd been in my shoes, walked the winding road of desperation, loneliness, and heartache, yet he'd made it out. He was a counselor in the psychiatric center, someone who helped people rather than hurt them. He was someone who made the world a better place rather than a more dangerous one, and I believed I could be too.

On a last note, I believe that in many ways I identified him with my father. He was a large, strong man, obviously a perpetrator in a world of perpetrators and victims, yet he was vulnerable and had himself been a victim. That lesson was powerful in my life because it convinced me that I didn't have to remain a victim. He showed me that although I'd been a victim in the past, it was my decision to remain one or not. I learned that day that you don't have to hurt people in order to not be a victim. That helping people was just as powerful, more so, than terrorizing them.

A few days later, a group of guys, Jared and Freddy and myself, decided that we were going to escape the psych ward. We devised a plan that was nearly foolproof. The idea was to escape when Joe brought us out to the courtyard for our hour of recreation time in the afternoon. We would be the first ones out, while Joe was always the last one, making certain everyone was accounted for.

Freddy was in front, then Jared, and finally me. The door opened, and we walked out as calmly as possible. Once outside, we turned right and bolted for the fence. Freddy leaped up, grabbing the bars that jutted from the top, and pulled himself up. Jared did the same, heaving himself up and over. I stood there, watching the pair, and in that moment, I heard a voice in my head telling me not to go. I hesitated and heard it again. *Don't go*, it said. *You need to get better.* My eyes welled, and I remained still as Jared landed on the other side.

"Hey! Get back here!" shouted Joe, making his way outside and around the corner.

Jared began running. Freddy was still struggling with the bars, pulling himself up until at last he was able to get one leg up and over. Then, disaster struck. His hand slipped, and he fell, slamming his ribs onto the bars. And then he rolled to the side and fell eight feet onto the ground, landing on his back.

"Ow!" he cried. "My ribs!" He held his ribs and rolled around on the ground.

Jared continued running until he could no longer be seen.

"That's it!" shouted Joe. "Everyone inside." He ushered us all back in through the door. We each took a seat in the main room, waiting to see what would happen to Freddy.

More adults stepped outside, and about twenty minutes later, Freddy was carried back inside on a stretcher, bandages wrapped all around his torso. We watched as he was carried off, and that would be the last time any of us would ever see him again. I'm not sure what happened to him.

For myself, I was glad I'd decided to stay. I met a teacher in the psych center who had a library full of books, and that was where I found my love of reading.

"Hey, Ms. T, can I take one of these books to my room with me?" I asked her one day in class after I'd finished my assignment.

"Sure you can, Junior. Just bring it back tomorrow," she said, smiling.

Aside from that, I'd also begun my doctor interviews. I was pulled into a conference room and sat at an oblong table, surrounded by ten doctors. They studied me, asking me questions about my life, my feelings, and my future. I didn't have a difficult time answering any of them until I thought about my future, of which I was clueless. I'd never spent much time thinking beyond the day, so to focus on anything long term was very difficult for me. I struggled through the series of questions and grew frustrated.

In the end they diagnosed me as bipolar, which back then was a big deal. It was a new diagnosis, and medications were still experimental, so they began experimenting on me right away. The next day I began taking meds, and that began the struggle to find myself because of the way the different medications would affect me. Some of them had no impact at all, while others turned me into a zombie. Nonetheless, I took my meds, continued reading, and stayed out of trouble, and after a month they were ready to release me back into the world. I was terrified and didn't want to leave.

Ten

STEPPING UP

Anyone who does anything to help a
child in his life is a hero to me.

—FRED ROGERS

When I was released from the psych center, my mom told me that she didn't want me at the house. Her boyfriend had been terrified when I'd pulled the gun on him, and now that I'd just been released from a psychiatric ward, he thought I just might be crazy enough to try and kill him. He gave my mother an ultimatum, either him or me, and she in turn gave me the mandate, "I want you out of my house."

It was then, in the eighth grade, that I began moving around from friend to friend, and I developed the two-week rule, something that would be a struggle for me until this day. I realized that at about two weeks, people get tired of you, and so I would stay with a friend for two weeks and then move on to the next friend. I continued doing that until I met a girl named Lori. We began dating, and I soon moved in with her and her family.

During this time I was experimenting with several different medications, none of which worked very well, and my behaviors were all over the place. I'm not certain how Lori put up with me as long as she did. All I can say is that she was the first person in my life who must have truly loved me because as difficult as I was, and I was as difficult as they came, she never judged me or lost interest. Soon after I stopped taking my meds altogether, the violence and mayhem in my life spiraled out of control.

I started hanging out with older guys all the time, and the drugs were easily accessible. I don't know if there was a single day, maybe one or two, when I didn't get high. I'd smoke with my friends, shower, and head back to Lori's house to have dinner with her and her family.

As grateful as I was to Lori and her family, seeing how they interacted made it difficult for me to stay there. They were a great family. Lori's mom, Stephanie, was up to that point the nicest woman I'd ever met. She was kind, thoughtful, and caring. She loved me, and although she had to have known that there were things going on in my life, she never made me feel judged in any way.

Lester, Lori's father, was a good man. The one challenge I had with him was that he was a drinker, and although he was always appropriate and generally a really nice guy, I couldn't help associating him with my father. That made it extremely difficult to let him into my life in the same way I was able to let Lori and Stephanie. That eventually caused a problem for me and would lead to the reason I had to move out.

The problem I had with them was that their lives only demonstrated for me how messed up I was. The more normal they were, the more like garbage I felt, and I hate to say that the worse I felt, the more miserable I made them. I couldn't understand why I was so angry all the time, and why that anger was aimed toward them, and I know I hurt them when they didn't deserve it. They'll never know it, but Lori and Stephanie were very special to me during one of the most difficult transitions I'd ever had—from the psych ward back into the real world. I don't know if I could have made the transition without their love and support.

I was in and out of trouble that year, still making a lot of mistakes and bad decisions. The one thing I did differently was to put more effort into making good grades in school. Joe's words stuck with me, and I believed that the way for me to have a different life was to follow his lead and "get smart." It wasn't long before I started to see the benefits of working hard on my grades.

I'd gotten kicked out of school again and sent to the alternative setting they called the guidance center. When I returned to school six weeks later, I ran into Sonja Stephens, my English teacher, on my first day back. She was standing out in the hallway in front of the door, snapping her fingers and tapping her foot. A song by The Doors was playing from her room, and we could hear the music as we approached. She was such a cool teacher.

"Hi, Junior," she said, welcoming me into class.

"Hi, Ms. Stephens," I replied, stepping in and finding my seat.

The bell rang and class soon started, with journaling. I had started on my assignment when Ms. Stephens called my name.

"Junior," she said, "can I see you out in the hallway?"

I nodded and rose to my feet, wondering what I'd done to get into trouble this time. I really had no idea because I liked Ms. Stephens and always tried to do what I was supposed to do in her class. I followed her out into the hallway. She stopped and turned to face me, holding a piece of paper up in the air. There was a large, red letter *A* circled in the middle of the sheet.

"Junior, you are a smart kid," she said. "Do you know what this is?"

I shook my head. "What is it?"

"This is the assignment I sent you while you were away in the guidance center," she replied.

I didn't know where she was going with this, and I was already uncomfortable with her telling me I was smart, and so I just stood there and waited.

"You made a perfect score on this work, Junior."

"It's not a big deal," I deflected. "I'm sure everybody did good on it," I said.

Ms. Stephens shook her head. "No one else got this assignment, Junior. I sent you an eleventh grade, AP English assignment from the high school. You scored perfectly on it."

I grew even more uncomfortable. I began to sweat, growing hot, and I had trouble making eye contact with her. She was telling me things that were the complete opposite of everything I believed about myself. Tears welled in my eyes, and I fought the urge to cry.

"You are a smart kid, Junior, but if you ever want to do anything with your life, you're going to have to get away from here. You're going to have to leave your family and friends, and go away, not just a little but a lot. You have to go all the way away, I'm talking a thousand miles away from here if you ever want your life to be different."

I didn't know what to do with what she was telling me, and so I grew angry and quiet. It wouldn't be until years later, a decade to be exact, that I would be able to say thank you. Ms. Stephens was the first person in my life to definitely prove to me that I had an ability to do well. What's even more interesting is that her words would prove to be prophesy in my life. She was right, it would take a distance no shorter than a thousand miles in order for me to be able to change the direction of my life. That comes later.

I entered high school not long after, and I was still making mistakes— robbing homes, stealing cars, selling drugs—but I continued to focus on my grades, thanks to Joe and Ms. Stephens. I also joined the freshman football team, and I met Coach Wilson, someone who became a very important man in my life. We had a love/hate relationship throughout my freshman year. I was a hardheaded kid who liked to do what I wanted, when I wanted. Coach Wilson was an old-school coach who believed kids should do what they were told, when they were told. We went back and forth throughout that year, arguing, disagreeing, and almost fighting with one another.

He went on to kick me off the team seven times that year, twice in one game. I played running back my freshman year, and the team pitched me the ball on a play. I ran around the edge of the defense and into the end zone to score a touchdown. When I returned to the sideline, Coach Wilson, still upset over an earlier disagreement we'd gotten into, told me to go sit in the stands. Furious, I took off all of my pads until I was standing in my undershirt and gray shorts, and I jumped the fence to sit in the stands.

Our defense made a big play, and we got the ball back two plays later. The sideline was hectic, and Coach Wilson yelled out, "Where's JR?"

The other students pointed into the stands, and when Coach Wilson turned and saw me, he shouted out, "What the hell are you doing up there? Get your ass down here!"

Excited, I jumped onto the field from the stands and quickly threw my pads back on. The very next play, I was back in the game with the ball, and I scored another touchdown. Smiling, I returned to the sidelines, where Coach Wilson said to me, "Get your ass back in the stands."

On another occasion he actually threatened to fight me. I was on the practice field goofing off while he was attempting to teach us a new play. He asked me to pay attention several times, and by the fourth or fifth time, he got so frustrated that he marched up and grabbed me by the face mask. He dragged me across three practice fields and into the main office, where he told me to sit down. I sat down and took off my helmet. I was furious. He'd just embarrassed me in front of the entire team.

I watched as he walked around his desk and went over to an old filing cabinet in the corner. He pulled one of the cabinets open and removed two pairs of 1950s leather boxing gloves. He turned and threw a pair at me. I caught them and dropped them on the desk in front of me. He sat in his chair and placed the other pair directly in front of himself. He was silently glaring at me when he reached up and removed his teeth! He pulled them all out of his mouth, gums, and everything, and he set them down on the desk, staring at me.

I've seen a lot of things in my life, but that terrified me. I squeezed the chair arms and leaned away from Coach Wilson.

"You want to fight me, boy?" he asked, his lips curved up and into his toothless mouth. "The way I see it, I have an advantage. My teeth are already gone, but you've got several I can knock out!"

I didn't want to fight Coach Wilson. He was the toughest man I knew. In a lot of ways, I compared him to my father in the same way I did with Joe. Coach Wilson was a tough, angry, and in some ways inappropriate man, much like my father as far as characteristics go. There was one major difference. I always eventually received approval from Coach, whereas my father had never given it to me.

After every major conflict Coach and I had, he would call the entire team together and have us circle up and join hands. He called it the circle of love, and I'll never forget the speeches he gave when we were in that circle. It was a special place, a sacred place, and each one of us would have given our lives to protect it.

"Boys, I did something yesterday I should never do. I broke the circle of love," he began. "Yesterday I came at one of our teammates, and I turned on him. That's not how we treat one another. That's not how you love a brother and a teammate. Each one of you should take care of one another, protect one another against anything that might come against you, and that includes me." He paused to look into each one of our eyes. "I failed you yesterday, and I ask for your forgiveness."

"We forgive you, Coach," I said.

He grinned and then frowned. "What is everyone standing around for? Get on the goal line. Time to run!"

Coach Wilson was an important man in my life. During a time of violence and inappropriate men in my life, he was a light. They don't make many men as special as him. I'm forever grateful to Coach Wilson, Joe, and Ms. Stephens for stepping up in my life.

Eleven

Sometimes your wrong choices bring you to the right places.

—SHANNON L. ALDER

My sophomore year was one of the most difficult years of my life. The drugs and violence became more extreme. I'd cut my fingertip off while working out in the gym, and so I didn't have football to keep me in line. I had constant access to any kind of drug I wanted, and anything I could put into my body, I did. I knew I was an addict when I found myself locked in a garage huffing paint thinner, trying to get high. I thought, *What am I doing here?* But I couldn't seem to quit, despite the fact that I knew what I was doing was destructive.

Aside from the drugs, the violence grew more extreme. I don't remember a time beyond fourth grade that I didn't fight. Fistfights were always straightforward—you hit them and they hit you until one of you gets knocked out or quits. Once that happened, the fight was over. But even fighting changed. I saw guys repeatedly kick another guy in the face long after he was unconscious. Fighting was no longer about proving a point or establishing a reputation. It was about hurting others as badly as possible.

It wasn't long after that I began carrying knives with me. I started cutting people. I got cut a few times myself. I didn't realize it at the time, but I was gradually walking myself into a life of danger and crime. I suppose I'd never been in a safe environment, but the level of danger and exposure to violence was steadily increasing. I simply adjusted so that I could continue to survive in my surroundings, and it took nearly losing my thumb in a fight to recognize the long-term consequences of my actions.

Of course we eventually began carrying guns, and before long I didn't go any place without at least one gun on me. There were several occasions when I shot at people, and I was shot at three times my sophomore year. I remember one night in particular when a friend of mine and I were out late at night in Peppertree Apartments, notorious for its drug dealing. We were chasing down some weed when we ran into a guy lighting up in the street. Long story short, there was a fight and a gun, bullets flying, and Sean and I running for our lives. I remember turning the corner in between buildings and hearing a bullet pass through the side bushes beside me.

The last time I had a run in with a gun, I was at a party, celebrating a victory by our football team. Instead of having a good time, I was in the front yard with my hands hanging loosely at my sides, a gun pointed at my forehead.

"Why you looking at my girl, bitch?" yelled Jose, his finger twitching about the trigger.

I stood there motionless, staring directly into his eyes. "I don't want no trouble, dog."

"You want trouble if you staring at my girl like that!" he yelled again.

I glanced to my side to see that the three guys I'd walked out with were gone. "I don't want no trouble, man," I repeated.

He looked uncertain for a moment, when his girlfriend, a girl I dated years before, tugged on his arm and whispered in his ear. He relaxed a bit. "Turn around and walk back in the house," he ordered me. "I better not see your face, or I'll put a hole in it."

I turned my back on him hesitantly and walked back to the house. I stepped inside, surrounded by drunk people laughing and doing drugs, smoking and snorting, dancing to the music that thumped in the background. I sat on a chair in the corner in shock and decided right then and there that I needed to do some things differently. What I was doing wasn't working, and the truth was, I didn't want to die.

If I'd have died right then, I would have been forgotten. My greatest fear is that the world will forget me when I'm gone. That, in the end, this place will be no different than it was before I got here. I didn't want to die; I wanted to live. I wanted my life to matter, to stand for something. I wanted this planet to be better because I existed. I wanted people to remember that I made a difference in their lives, but up until that point in my life, I hadn't done anything with the gifts I was given. Part of the problem was I couldn't see the gifts I had, and part of the problem was I didn't know how to be any different than I was. The desire was there, but the know-how wasn't.

There are so many kids out there in the same types of situations I was in, kids who were born down on their luck, who long to make a difference, to live a significant life, but have absolutely no idea how to do it. They need people to show them the way, just like I needed them. Without people to show them, to show me the way, there quite literally is no hope, and no chance for us to succeed.

I left that party depressed and overwhelmed with a sense of hopelessness. I still saw myself as a victim to my circumstances, and so the thought of being able to change my life on my own was daunting. It felt impossible, especially since everyone around me was in the same circumstances and living the same type of life that I was.

I went into my junior year of high school determined to do the best I could to be different. I finally made the varsity football team, and I decided to use that as a platform for the differences I wanted to see. I spent every waking hour in the gym, running in the park late at night, anything I could do to get better. It was great for me because I was able to see the results on the field, but all the work kept me busy and too tired to get into trouble. It was amazing to see different results, and for the first time in my life, I felt encouraged that maybe things could be different.

It wouldn't be long before all that hope was stolen from me. I was sitting in class on a Thursday, acting up, cracking jokes, trying to get attention from my classmates. The door opened and two officers with HPD, the Houston Police Department, walked into the room. They approached my teacher and the next thing I knew, both officers were standing in front of my desk.

"We need you to stand up," said one of the officers.

"Me?" I asked.

"Please stand up now," repeated the officer.

I rose to my feet. One of the officers turned me to the side and pulled my hands behind my back. They put me in handcuffs in front of all my classmates and marched me out of the school and into a squad car. We then drove down to Harris County lockup, and I was thrown into the holding tank there. I was the youngest person there, and when a man, obviously an addict, sat down and asked what gang I was with, I realized I'd thrown everything away.

Twelve

The Power of One

Darkness cannot drive out darkness; only light can do that. Hate cannot drive out hate; only love can do that.

—Martin Luther King Jr.

I was released from jail and charged with a felony assault and battery with intent to do harm. I was put on probation, ordered to complete hundreds of hours of community service, and to pay back thousands of dollars in restitution. It was a sad time in my life because I was forced to accept that I was no better than my father and his family. My mother had always told me I was just like my dad, that evil flowed through my veins, and now the felony was proof that she was right.

I went back to school my senior year to play football. I desperately needed to be a part of a team, and I was drawn to the success. It was that year that I met a teacher who would change my life forever. I signed up for a class called "teen leadership," and on the first day of school, the teacher was standing in the hallway, shaking kids' hands as they approached. I was surprised to see her reach out to shake my hand. Every teacher on campus knew I was a convicted felon, so not many of them wanted contact with me. I took her hand and introduced myself as Stanley, the first time in my life I'd ever done so.

Stanley was my father's name, and I'd hated my father for a long time. I didn't realize it at the time, but that decision to take ownership of my name, to recognize that I wasn't my father, was a massive step for me on the road to self-discovery. I entered her classroom, and for the first time, I found an adult who was willing to be the role model I'd been searching for my entire life.

It's not that I didn't have appropriate adults in my life, because I did. It's just that none of them were willing or able to invest the amount of time I needed in order to begin changing my behaviors. It's one thing to encourage a kid; it's another thing entirely to help a kid change. It takes not only encouragement but relentless love, uncompromising consistency, and stern accountability.

Monda Simmons, my teacher, stood at the door every day, welcoming students into class. We always started by sharing good things that were happening in our lives and then had an opportunity to journal about various topics, all very relevant to our lives. She taught us skills like how to reframe situations, to take negative circumstances and find the positive in them. Seems simple enough, but for many of the students, myself included, it was the first time we'd ever searched for the good in life. She taught us listening skills and conflict-resolution strategies, all lessons that applied immediately to our daily lives.

The best thing was that she actually believed that we could learn those topics, even though some of them were difficult. She motivated us by sharing that many of the strategies were used in corporate America, and we were all determined to be successful because she believed in us. She wasn't really a touchy-feely person, though she was very affirming and encouraging, but we never doubted that she loved us. For students like myself, the bigger lesson was that if she loved me, I must be lovable. It took a while, but I finally began to believe that, and once I did, everything changed for me.

I still struggled with who and what I saw when I looked in the mirror. There was still this ugly, trailer-trash kid looking back at me, but Monda's reflection was now looking over my shoulder, smiling down on me, saying, "I believe in you." It was enough to light within me a fire to do better and to be better. Three months into the school year, I asked Monda if I could talk to her before class. She said yes, and the following morning I showed up early.

"Good morning, Mrs. Simmons," I greeted her.

"Good morning, Stanley. How are you doing?" she replied.

"I'm good. How are you?"

"Wonderful, I'm wonderful," she said. "Is everything all right?"

I smiled. "Yes, ma'am, everything is all right. I just wanted to ask you something."

She smiled back. "Well, OK. What can I do for you?"

I took a deep breath, feeling the tears already welling up in my eyes, and began. "Mrs. Simmons, I don't want to be who I am anymore. You've showed me that I can be something more, something better, and that's what I want. The problem is that I don't know how to be anything other than what I am. This life is all that I know." I took another deep breath and continued. "But I know you, and I see how you are all the time, and I know you know how to have a different kind of life, the kind of life I want mine to look like. So here's what I need from you. I need a list. I need you to tell me what I need to do for my life to look like yours, and I'll do it, no questions asked. Whatever you put on the list I'll do, but please, just make me a list. Just help me."

I was crying then. She rose from her seat and came around the desk to hug me.

"Of course I'll help you," she said, pulling back from me and staring me in the eyes, her hands pressed against my shoulders. "You know I believe in you, don't you?"

"I know," I replied.

The following day Mrs. Simmons had a list ready to go for me. It consisted of small behavioral changes: sit in the front of class, show up to class early, ask at least two questions each class, show up for tutoring in the morning, and so on. As promised, I followed the list, no questions asked, and not only did my grades begin to improve, but also my relationships with other kids and teachers improved. I felt like the model student, and by the end of the year, I'd earned a four-point-zero GPA my senior year. It was such a shock that I thought they'd given me the wrong report card. They hadn't. It was mine.

I finished the year with a full-ride football scholarship to Saint Xavier University in Chicago. I'd been living with my grandparents up until that point, but I found out my mother had gotten into some trouble and was living in a motel room. As much as I wanted to go to college, I couldn't leave with her in that situation, so I turned down my scholarship and took on a job as a welder.

Without my knowing, Mrs. Simmons had contacted the university and spoken with the president, Dr. Yanikowski, as well as the Sisters of Mercy and explained the situation I'd found myself in. She spoke on my behalf, pleading with them to find a way to help me, and sure enough, they did! The university agreed to use the scholarship monies to hold my place on the football team as long as I resumed my scholarship in the spring. So that's what I did. I welded for six months and made my way to Chicago.

I would be remiss here if I didn't mention the outpouring of support I received from different people in getting me to Chicago. The Kitchen Angels from Round Top, Texas, in particular, were amazing. They conducted quilting fundraisers and started a *Stanley Fund* to raise money for winter clothes for me. They would later help me during times of dire need as well. Without them my journey to Chicago would have been much more difficult. It took an entire community to help me get where I was supposed to be, but it all started with just one teacher.

I was involved in everything at Saint Xavier, and in an effort to not list my résumé right here, we'll just say I graduated magna cum laude with an English literature degree. I went on to earn my master's in educational leadership, and I began keynote speaking for the Flippen

Group, the same company that created the teen leadership class I met Mrs. Simmons in.

I'm extremely grateful to Mrs. Simmons for the love, patience, and kindness she showed me as a teacher and the unrelenting desire to see me succeed that she demonstrated in helping me get to college. We now work together as teammates and it is from this platform that I began the next chapter in my life—the journey to find my father.

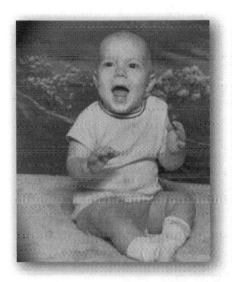

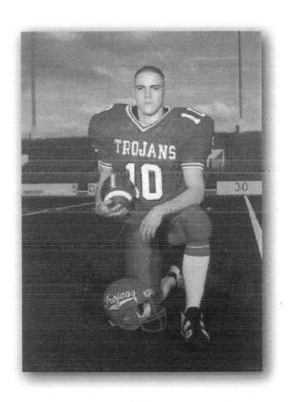

Stanley Leone Jr.

Thirteen

Nothing in life is to be feared, it is only to be understood. Now is the time to understand more, so that we may fear less.

—MARIE CURIE

That day was filled with a mixture of emotions. I was excited, a little curious, and a little afraid. I was on my way to see my father for the first time in 25 years. To be honest, I'd just about written him off. There was a time in my life when all that mattered to me was finding him. I didn't think it would be difficult to do, and I was determined to put closure to my memories of him. I had no idea how hard it was to find someone who didn't want to be found.

In today's world, with access to the Internet, finding him should have been easy. I should have known better. Nothing in my life has ever been easy. The only thing I knew about my father was that he was born in Zwolle, Louisiana, and so that was where I decided to start.

I checked my schedule and realized I would be speaking to several groups of high school kids in Longview, Texas, and Zwolle was a rather short drive away. I'm not sure why, but that short drive seemed to turn into one that took forever. My mind was consumed with pieces of my own story, as I relived the speech from that morning over and over again. It's a strange thing when you're in the business of telling your own story, with its unique hurts and pains, to impact the lives of others. No speech ever ends up the same. They always end up focusing on a different aspect of the "family album." As if during each speech, there are only certain pages that have an impact on any particular audience.

Sometimes those pages are consumed with stories of my dad and the few clear memories I have of him. Sometimes the pages are about my mom, her struggles and pains and attempts to keep our family together. Other times the pages are filled with memories and feelings of what it was like to be poor, moving around all the time, living in motels, or in my mom's station wagon. At other times, when the pain of an audience is palpable, the pages are filled with dark messages about the rape, a life of violence, being institutionalized, or being a convicted felon.

I never really know what to expect when I step on stage, and I think it's better that way. I've gone into speaking opportunities with a preset notion of what it will be, and I've even tried to stick to the script in order to make my message fit my plan. Those have turned out to be the worse experiences I've had on stage. It's much better to have no agenda, to completely release myself to the potential of everything, and to hold fast to the desire to be open to the needs of the people I'm there to help.

I'm not sure I can explain it, but after speaking I often feel a spiritual and emotional weight that wasn't there beforehand. Although I wasn't aware of it most of my career, I realized I needed a therapist to help me process the personal impact of reliving the memories for the benefit of others. He told me the messages were a form of controlled flashing back, similar to posttraumatic stress disorder, and that I had never understood nor properly dealt with that baggage. But back to the journey at hand...

Before I knew it, I'd passed a sign welcoming me into Sabine Parish, the very parish my father grew up in. A sense of electric excitement filled me as I rolled up on the sign announcing Zwolle, and I slowed to a snaillike pace as I realized the town was nothing more than a concrete road that cut through shacks dispersed throughout wooded acres of land.

I guess I've never been really good at planning, and I had no plan for what I would do when I arrived. I just knew it was a trip I had to make, I needed to make, so I sat there in my car on the shoulder of the road. My life has been a series of unplanned events that seem to lead me to my next step, and sitting there, my next step was clear as a patrol car pulled up in front of me.

I got out of the car, and with my hands held in the air in front of me, I approached the window of the patrol car. I don't recommend doing this when pulled over, but I needed help! I don't know if you are familiar with police officers in Louisiana, especially backwoods Louisiana, but they are a paranoid bunch, operating in very rural areas concentrated with a volatile population. I kept my distance as his window rolled down about halfway.

"Can I help you, boy?"

"Yes, sir. This may sound kind of funny to you, but I just drove in from Longview, and I'm looking for my father. I have no idea where to start. I know this is a long shot, but Dad was in trouble with the cops all the time, so I thought I had a pretty good chance asking for your help."

He chuckled under his breath. "That doesn't sound so weird to me if he's had trouble with the law. I've worked Zwolle for years now, and if he's here and has been in trouble, then I'll know him."

"Well, his name's Stan Leone, and I know he grew up here. I don't think he's here anymore, but I thought the best place to start would be at the beginning. You ever heard of the Leones?"

He was silent for a moment, pondering what I'd just told him. "Boy, I don't know if your father is here or not, but I do know the Leone clan. In fact, if you make a left down that road right there, there's a bar about a mile or so down, and the Leones own it."

A surge of hope rushed through me. He pointed at the turnoff directly across from where I'd pulled over on the shoulder. Like I said, unplanned events that get me to where I'm supposed to be.

"Thank you, sir. I'll drive out there and see if I can find anything." I turned away and headed to the car when he shouted back at me.

"You be careful out there. Good luck to you."

That was the first step in a long, winding path of discovery for me. I drove to the bar, and upon entering I quickly came to terms with the fact that I was a definite outsider and the center of everyone's attention. It felt like one of those movies when a stranger walks into a crowded bar and the talking stops, the music stops, and all eyes are on the new guy.

That was the beginning of a series of events that would eventually change my life and lead me where I was that day, boarding that plane, heading to California, ready for a final confrontation with a ghost from my past. How much pain they have cost us, the mistakes of our fathers and of their fathers, and so on? The past cannot be undone, but if faced with courage and a forgiving heart, it need not be repeated.

The ticket agent at my boarding gate interrupted my thoughts. "Boarding pass, sir." She didn't even look up as she asked for my ticket. To her, I was another passenger heading to another destination. For me, this plane and this destination was one of the biggest moments of my life.

"Yes, ma'am. Here you go. How are you?"

"Boarding pass, sir," she said to the next passenger.

Fourteen

FLYBY MEMORIES

*The bitterest tears shed over graves are for words
left unsaid and deeds left undone.*

—UNKNOWN

A first-class upgrade is always a nice start to any three-and-a-half-hour trip. I settled into the plush leather recliner, buckled my seatbelt, and waited for the bell to ring, notifying passengers it was safe to use electronics. I put my headphones on and turned on my phone. I knew thousands of thoughts would be racing through my mind, and I needed the flight time to find the courage to face my father when I landed.

The haunting roll of Andrea Bocelli crept into my ear, sliding through my canal and winding its way into the inner recesses of thought. I let Andrea sing me into a wakeful sleep, conscious of everything around me but disconnected from anything in that moment. The beautiful harmony of his voice, the depth of his lyrics, and the strength of his notes powered through the locks and chains that sealed every door of the inner rooms of my heart and mind. Now, these hidden doors were open, and memories that were more real than the seat I was sitting in danced to the lullaby he serenaded me with. It was a peaceful place to find rest, and I returned to the recollection of my uncle.

I'd left Zwolle with a phone number for an uncle no one had heard from in years. His name was Henry, and it was the first I'd heard of him. The story was that he was wanted by law enforcement in multiple states and was hiding out. Being a twelve-time convicted felon tends to make a person a bit paranoid, I'm sure. Although I was filled with disappointment because the Longview trip hadn't panned out the way I had hoped, I was undeterred in my resolve to locate my father and hopefully close that chapter in my life.

After I had landed and got a good night's sleep, I called Henry the next day and, after getting an automated voice mail, left him a message. I did the best I could to explain who I was and what I was doing, but it was difficult to express the emotions I felt. Nothing prepares you for the feelings a task like locating an abusive father who abandoned you over twenty years earlier brings out. I was afraid of so many things, and the fact that I would be meeting this stranger, this violent stranger, in the middle of nowhere, wasn't lost on me.

To my surprise, Henry called back that day. I remember seeing the number, and although the area code was different from most calls I received, somehow I knew it was him. Hesitantly, I answered the phone.

"Hello. This is Stanley."

"Who is this?"

"This is Stanley. Who is this?"

"I believe I'm your uncle Henry. I'm your daddy's brother."

There was a moment of silence, like someone had just been pronounced dead, an eerie silence, and then I spoke.

"Thanks for calling back. I wasn't sure you would."

"I could tell you were who you said you were. You sound just like Stanley."

I can't explain the rush of emotion, the sense of pain, and for some odd reason, the feeling of guilt at hearing someone say I was similar to my dad. For all my life, I'd hated him. I blamed him for everything that went wrong in my life. I blamed him for the constant unhappiness that plagued me no matter how many successes I experienced. I blamed him for the restlessness in my marriage, the discontent with what I was doing and had done up until that point with my life.

The mind is a strange thing. It is a wondrous thing how the brain attempts to rationalize irrational experiences with traumatic emotional responses. Such a dichotomy takes place: a sense of hatred toward those who perpetrate violence and harm on you yet also a dumbfounding longing to have those same perpetrators in your life. The human soul can find itself in the midst of a war, wanting with everything in it to be different and separated from the very thing you long to be reunited with.

"I do? I sound like him?"

"Just like your daddy. He had a voice just like yours. Have you found him?"

"No. I'm trying to locate him, but he's pretty tough to get in contact with. I haven't heard from him, and apparently no one else has either. It's like he just fell off the face of the earth. Like he dropped out of existence. I only got your number from your cousin Joe, who still lives in Zwolle, and he didn't even know if it was the right one."

"Yeah, little Joey. He ain't so little anymore, is he?"

I laughed. "No. He's not real tall, but he's a pretty stocky guy. When I showed up at the bar where I met Joey, he was out back, sitting on the tailgate of a truck. I felt like I was walking into one of the old *Godfather* movies."

"Yeah, that's Joey. He and his brother never left Zwolle. Yeah, I been looking for your daddy too. I made a vow to myself that I would find him again before I died. Don't take this the wrong way, but Stanley and I didn't exactly part on the best terms."

I was uncomfortable with him referring to my dad as Stanley. Everyone I'd ever met called him Stan, and that's why I went by Stanley. I guess, in an effort to bring a distinct break between myself and him, I made Stanley *my* name. I even dropped the "junior" designation. I simply didn't want to be second to a man I felt I was different from and better than.

"No offense taken. Those things happen. Have you been able to find him, or at least get into contact with him?"

"No. I've tried, pulled a few last-known addresses and phone numbers from the phone book, but he's never been at any of them. I want to find him though. I promised myself I would because I want him to know I never had no ill will toward him. I always loved your daddy. He was my little brother, and I never meant for us to part the way we did."

There was another silence on the phone. I could feel it drifting through the receiver, slithering up to choke me when he spoke again.

"I'd like to meet you. Just like to see you. We're blood, you know. Me and your daddy was real close. We did everything together for a while there. Him, me, and Wayne. That's your other uncle, Wayne. You're my blood, your daddy was my brother, so I love you like you was my own."

Emotion gripped my heart and twisted it in a fist of agony. I'd tried for years to dissociate from Dad and his family. I tried to pretend he was a story, like the one I shared on stage every week, one of horrible tragedy, of violence, abuse, alcohol, and rage. The scenes that replayed in my head were scenes from movies I'd seen. I wanted to believe I couldn't be from the same stock he was. I needed to believe I was from a different breed, a better pedigree, yet at the same time, I was aware of the very real longing to be reconciled with the blood that flowed through our family's veins. Separation was vital to my identity, for I always feared, as Nietzsche declared, "What was silent in the father speaks in the son, and often I found in the son the unveiled secret of the father."

"That would be good. I'd like to meet you too. Maybe I could ask you some questions? Maybe you could tell me a little about our family? I don't even know my grandma's name."

"Her name was Alice. Your grandma was a good lady. Never hurt nobody. Use to tell us the best stories when we was little. And your grandpa was Walter. He was a good man, a hard man. Didn't take much off nobody either. Not your grandpa. But he was a good man."

"Yeah. I think we should meet. I have a lot of questions. I haven't seen Dad since I was 5."

"I remember you when you were just a little one. Yeah, you were a little bitty ole thing. Your daddy loved you too, used to dote on you and say you were his boy. That's why you're his namesake. Gave you his name and everything because he thought the world of you."

"Can you meet next week? I'll make another drive out that way when my schedule brings me home for a bit."

"Any time you like. I ain't got much going on here. Just tell me where you want to meet. I'll drive my old car wherever I need to. You're my blood, and I love you like you're my own."

"Just give me your address, and I'll GPS it."

He laughed under his breath. "I don't think no map can get you here. Just head out to Alexandria and call me when you get there. I'll come out to meet you."

A heavy stream of worry poured through my thoughts, cutting through the canyons of false confidence and pretend calm. I knew I had to put a stop to the fear before, like a floodgate bursting at the seams, it rushed through my flimsy barricades and overwhelmed me with indecision and cowardice. I sought refuge in the words of Robert Louis Stevenson: "You cannot run away from weakness; you must sometimes fight it out or perish; and if that be so, why not now, and where you stand?"

Courage swelled in my chest, and I was overwhelmed with a sudden rattling that clattered my teeth. As I stirred from my restless escape, the flight attendant informed me, "As you can see, we are experiencing turbulence. For your own safety, please remain seated until the captain turns off the fasten-seatbelt sign. Thank you."

Fifteen

UNCLE HENRY

I don't like to commit myself about heaven and hell—you see, I have friends in both places.

—MARK TWAIN

It wasn't long before I was on my way. I was soon in Louisiana, closer than I'd ever been to finding my father. I drove down a winding path through what seemed like a forest reserve for hours. I didn't even remember when I'd crossed the state line into Louisiana, but I had, and I was well on my way to Alexandria. I didn't know how smart or how dumb I was being, driving out into the middle of nowhere to meet a man I'd never met, but there I was.

Twelve felonies aren't exactly the same as "I made a mistake." This was a habitually violent man, and as I got closer to the meeting point, I was more thankful by the minute that I'd told my wife where I was going and who I was meeting. Family or not, violence is a ruthless thing that crosses all lines and knows no boundaries. Truth be said, tough as I thought I was, I was afraid.

We met at an old gas station in the middle of nowhere. No parking lots. No dealerships. No grocery stores. No buildings. Of course, in my mind, that meant no witnesses! I sat in my rental car, windows up and doors locked, and made the call to Henry. He said he and my aunt Charlotte would be there in fifteen minutes. The only exciting thing about that was, I knew wherever he took me, it would only be fifteen minutes away. How bad could it be?

Fifteen minutes later (to the second), an old beat-up station wagon, which, quite frankly, looked like it was on its last wheel, pulled into the gravel stop area. My heart fluttered, and my mouth was dry. My pulse sped up, and I was suddenly seized with hot flashes and cold sweats. If I hadn't known any better, and clearly I didn't, I'd have sworn I was having a panic attack! The old car came to a stop twenty feet away. My phone rang.

"Hello. This is Stanley." I always answered like I was on the job.

"This is your uncle. You here?"

"Yeah. You're in a station wagon?"

"Yeah. I'm getting out now. It's me and your aunt Charlotte. I'll see you in a minute."

The phone went dead. *What the hell am I doing?* I thought. I mean really, what was I hoping to accomplish, and why hadn't I brought someone with me? Maybe someone like Denzel Washington from *Man on Fire*, or someone who could cause some serious damage if I needed them to! Instead, I was there all alone.

Then a funny thing happened. In the midst of my overwhelming fear, a calculated calm came over me, and the calloused attitude that I had cultivated in my life on the streets of Houston jump-started survival instincts and I was ready to meet him. *What the hell was I scared of? He's not the only convicted felon here!*

He was a lanky man, long arms, long legs, and a short torso. Standing about 5'10" and weighing about 150 pounds soaking wet, I quickly assessed the situation and concluded that I could seriously hurt him if I had to defend myself. The initial engagement was a bit awkward, him being a hardened man in his sixties and me being an eager twenty-something-year-old with a predictable knack for hugging. He put his hand out stiffly, and I bypassed it, grabbing him up in a full embrace. He hugged me back, gently and in an unsure way to begin with, but it steadily grew into a lingering and warm embrace.

I stepped back from him and sized him up again. Yep, 5'10", about 150 pounds, old, and weakened. I, on the other hand, was in good shape at the time. All 214 pounds sat densely on my 5'10" frame, and there was no doubt in my mind he would be misguided if he thought he could take advantage of me in any way. I smiled and, in a second or two, took him in. His jeans were old, tight, and dirty. They hugged his rail-thin legs and draped down over a pair of worn work boots. He wore a fitted country-western long-sleeved shirt and a blue jean jacket over it. His hands were restricted in a neutralized position at the moment, pressed firmly into his pockets.

Glancing over his shoulder to the old car, I noticed my aunt's frame in the passenger seat, face pressed against the windshield, trying to get a better view. She waved emphatically through the window. I smiled and lifted my hand in a greeting. Uncle Henry looked back.

"That's your aunt Charlotte. She's real excited to meet you."

"I'm glad we could meet. How far away do you live?"

"Not too far. You can just get in the car and ride with us if you like."

Instinct kicked in. "No, I have a rental car right there."

"That's OK. You can just leave it here. They know me here. No one will mess with it, and I'll drive you back up when you're ready to go to get it."

Tricky situation. Of course I wasn't going anywhere unless I was in control of how I got there and when I left. Rule number one: never give up control. The tricky part was saying it in a way that didn't offend him. It was our first meeting, and we were family, so I wanted to be sure to not destroy any signs of bonding we might have had. I thought about it, *What can I lose? I'll just tell him the truth.*

"I appreciate it, Uncle Henry. I have my car right here, and I'm not too sure about where we're going. Why don't I just follow you, and I'll save you the trip from having to drive me back out here when it's time to go."

To my surprise he immediately deferred. "OK. That sounds good too. I won't drive too fast. Just stay behind me because you can get lost out here."

We hugged again, and he turned and went to his car, and relieved, I turned and went to my car. As we pulled out, I can't begin to express the intensity of prayer I entered into on that fifteen-minute drive back to his place. I prayed for safekeeping, a good meeting, for their hearts to be softened, for my car to not break down, no flats, and a safe return!

So the road I followed him on wasn't exactly what one might call a road. I couldn't tell you how to get there today if my life depended on it! All I know is we drove between trees, through gravel, and in dirt the entire way there. With no mailing address, I understood now why it was so difficult to get in touch with this man. My understanding of how people can just "disappear" deepened.

Don't get me wrong; I'm no geographical whiz to begin with, but I tried with everything in me to remember an escape route if I needed to get out of there in a hurry. Shamefully I thought about every possible scenario, even down to what I would tell the cops if I had to defend myself.

"Yes, sir, officer. I came out to interview him for a book I am writing about my father and what he did to my family as a kid, and he got offended and tried to attack me. Being out in the middle of nowhere, I didn't have an opportunity to escape and had no other choice but to defend myself." Oh yeah, I had every possible situation mapped out in my head—except for the one that happened.

On what would be the final turn off, we pulled into a clearing with what looked like an old tool shack sitting alone in the middle of a field of overgrown grass. The roof was slightly caved in, and shingles were intermixed with old sheets of plywood. Two windows on either side of the door were sealed up with foil, and the door itself was handcrafted (and I'm not talking catalogue-crafted either!).

Hesitant at first, Henry and I sat at a small card table set up in the kitchen, and he unfolded a chair for me.

"Would you like some coffee?"

Another unspoken rule: Always accept a drink or something to eat when it's offered to you. If you say no, you run the risk of appearing like you think you're too good to eat or drink what they have. Never take seconds because people usually don't have enough to warrant offering you something in the first place. "Sure, I'll have a cup."

The ceiling sat low at about seven feet, and the place seemed dark and damp. There was what I considered to be the living room, which ran into the kitchen, where the table was set up. An old couch was the only piece of furniture. The kitchen led into the only bedroom. I never made it back there to see it, but if it was anything like the rest of the house, I assume it was just about empty.

I've grown up poor. I've moved around so many times I've lost count. We've lived in government housing that was condemned and knocked down by the city construction crew. We've lived in motel rooms and even in my mom's station wagon for a while. But Uncle Henry and Aunt Charlotte lived in the worse conditions I'd ever been exposed to. It was third-world status.

He walked over with a cup for me and one for himself. Charlotte pulled up a chair to the right of Henry and sat with us.

"You want sugar?"

"Sure, I'll take a bit." I poured a moderate amount to sweeten the coffee and passed it back to Uncle Henry. He reached out for it and poured some into his cup. He kept pouring. And kept pouring. Then poured some more, to the point when I thought the coffee would spill over the rim of his cup. He liked his sugar with a little flavor of coffee! I took a quick moment to glance at Charlotte.

The first thing that came to mind was heroin. I knew she was definitely a drug addict, and from the amount of sugar Henry was still pouring into his coffee, he was too. She was haggard, face drawn tight and sagging at the same time. Her hair was a disheveled mess of sandy-blond locks that seemed to parade on her head. Both of them had lost their teeth some time ago, and she slouched over the table with her weight on her elbows like gravity sat painfully on her shoulders. Either Henry had enough sugar or he ran out. Whichever the case, the pouring stopped.

He wasn't anything like I expected. We spent a lot of time laughing and talking about trivial things like fighting, his childhood, and the ghost stories my grandmother used to tell him as a boy.

"She'd get to making that low rumble in her throat and a scary voice and she'd scare the hell out of us!"

He would then tell me about growing up in Zwolle. "There wasn't much of nothing out here. We had a town with a grocery mart and a post office, but that's about it. Wasn't nothing but dirt roads and one lawman. He was a real cowboy too, used to ride his horse up and down those roads with a big old cowboy hat and all. Wasn't no uniform either. He wore jeans and a flannel shirt that would button down, and he had a little star pinned right here"—he motioned to his heart—"on his chest."

I was pulled into Henry and his stories of a forgotten childhood. He spoke about it with such freedom and such a lightness that, if I hadn't known better, I could have believed he had as good a childhood as anyone could.

"We didn't have no TV back then neither. We didn't get electricity in this town until the late fifties, so we would use these kerosene lanterns and the fire to see where we was going and what we was doing. Momma used to take us out on the porch real late at night, when it was dark and you could see every one of them stars up there, and she would sit in this old rocker and tell us stories about the goblins in the woods.

"There was woods all around us, but Daddy owned the land we was on. Back then, in Zwolle, you didn't have to sign for nothing or pay for nothing. All you had to do was, if you see some land you want, you go and take it. You just build your house on it and fence off what you want and it was yours. So Daddy fenced off some land for us and all around us was the woods, and Momma would sit us around outside and tell us all about the goblins that would get you if you went out into the woods after dark. We didn't much believe her, but it was real scary to listen to her tell it. We spent all our time in the woods though."

"Who? You and my dad?"

"All of us. You see, there was two generations of Leones. Daddy was married twice. He married my momma first. They had 5 of us: Joe, Jared, Ruby, Gertrude, and me. Then Daddy left my momma, and he got with another woman. And they had your daddy, Wayne, and Earl.

"There's a lot more of us Leones running around too, but don't none of us know each other. Daddy had a lot of kids. There was about twentysomething years difference between some of us, so we was all different ages. I wasn't much older than your daddy, maybe eight years, so I was with him and Wayne a lot. We would go to those woods and have fighting matches."

"Fighting matches?"

"Yeah, you know. Fighting matches. We would get some old socks and put them on, and then if you wanted a piece of one of your brothers, you would tell him and y'all would go at it. Your daddy was tough. Couldn't nobody whoop him, not even the older ones. They tried, but he was fast. He'd hit you and be behind you before you knew he hit you! Only one could have probably given him a fight was your uncle Jared, but he went away when we was all real young. I'm in touch with him. I tracked him down in Florida. Different last name now, but he's a Leone too."

"Everyone had told me Dad was tough," I said to my uncle. "They said when he was drinking, you didn't want to mess with him much."

"Yeah, he was tough. Couldn't no one take him." His focused seemed to drift as he spoke, no doubt reflecting on memories made several lifetimes ago, and there was a tender mourning quality to his voice.

"I really hate the way your daddy and me parted."

"Tell me about it."

We went on to talk for several hours. To be honest, I lost track of time. I was so enamored with the zeal he told stories with, the vividness he recollected the memories that seemed to flood his mind all at once, that not once did I glance down to check the time. I learned so much sitting with my father's brother.

I learned that Grandpa Walter was a bootlegger, and his specialty was a corn liquor called "white lightning." In those days, bigotry and segregation still colored the boundaries drawn among men, and the black quarter is where Walter made most of his money.

"He would go on down to n*-town and call them out: 'Here, n*. Heeeere, n*. Come get it.' And them black folks would come running for that lightning. They called your grandpa Mr. White Head because he had a head of long white hair that would go down to the middle of his back. They would come out every time he got a new batch and drink it up before he left.

"Sometimes he would stay there with them and drink and then charge them for whatever they used. It was funny to see him drink up all that lightning and then them blacks didn't want to pay, so he'd go to town on them. Most of them though never gave him no trouble. Daddy took care of a couple of them, and after that they never gave him no trouble."

I'm not sure what "took care of them" meant, but I didn't ask. I just nodded and listened and imagined the worse.

"Daddy would make us drink too. I been drinking that lightning since I was about 5 years old. He said it's what men did, and he would call each one of us in and tell us to drink it; we were becoming men. And you better drink that lightning when Daddy told you to! I didn't want to drink it once. I didn't like it at all—kind of burned, you know, like drinking straight vodka or something—and I cried and told Daddy I didn't want it."

Henry leaned over, laying his face flat on the table while he continued talking, parting his wiry hair.

"See them scars? If you didn't drink it, Daddy would tell you, 'You better drink it, boy!' and if you didn't, he would get this old PVC pipe he had laying around, you know, for plumbing and stuff, and he would hit you upside the head with it. He split me wide open right here (he gestured to a long, jagged scar staining the complexion of his scalp behind his left ear), and I drank it the next time he told me." Henry laughed a bit at the memory as he was lifting his head.

"Was he tough on you guys?"

"Yeah, Daddy was hard. He was all right if you did what he thought you should be doing, but for the most part, he was tough."

We went back and forth; I'd ask questions, and he'd tell me story after story like this. Although I've heard conflicting stories, Henry told me about his daddy getting into a fight with one of his brothers and shooting him. I'm not sure if the brother died of the gunshot wound or not, but I'm fairly certain the fight and gun incident took place. It must have been a scary place to be, knowing your own father wouldn't hesitate to shoot you if he saw the need.

With only one "lawman" in town, legal consequences weren't much of a worry, especially since there seemed to be more Leone boys in town than there were any other people. I also found out that Stan and Henry had gotten into a fight the last time they'd seen each other.

"One time, that son of a bitch, Wayne, was with your daddy out drinking. They had a couple of girls with them, and I guess Wayne thought he was gonna come get some money from me. So he drove here with your daddy and those two girls in the car."

"I was asleep with your aunt Charlotte, and we had a little one in the house. And it was maybe two or three in the morning when I heard Wayne outside honking his car horn and cussing at me from outside. 'You better go on, Wayne,' I said. 'You better get out of here,' and he kept going on about money I owed him. They knew I had just gotten some money from a run of drugs I did, and I guess he thought he was go'n test me and thought he could better me.

"Anyway, he kept on yelling and making all this noise, so I went outside to tell him to leave. I had a baby sleeping in the house. I came out with my .22 rifle and told him to get out of there. But Wayne was always stupid, biggest baby of all of us, but your daddy was always protecting him, and he started coming at me, saying he was gone get my money. I pointed it right at his chest, and I woulda shot him too, but your daddy grabbed that rifle and pointed it down.

"We started fighting. Wayne trying to act tough, and I ended up pulling the trigger. I didn't know the barrel was sitting on your daddy's leg. Right there on his left groin area. I put a hole right through the leg. The shot blew it all to pieces. The next thing I know, your daddy looks like he's bleeding to death, and I tell Wayne to get him out of there. They jumped in that car, and those two girls was screaming and all. And I guess he took your daddy to the hospital.

"That was the last time I saw your daddy. I sure wish I could see him again. I ain't got no bad will toward him. It's Wayne I would kill. He was always stupid. That's why he's where he's supposed to be right now—locked away for the rest of his life."

Aunt Charlotte started to move for the first time since we began talking and actually looked interested. I looked at her, and Henry started speaking again.

"Your aunt Charlotte writes to Wayne. I say a few words in the letters sometime myself. I figure he ain't got nobody else that writes to him. I send him money sometime too, so he can get his essentials, you know, soap, a toothbrush, toothpaste. But he ain't never getting out."

Some of what I heard was expected, but some of it was so off the wall I didn't know if he was making it up as he went. He told me he and Charlotte had been together almost thirty years in spite of her cheating on him with Wayne. For your wife to have an affair with your brother is not a good thing but trivial in the larger scheme of things they'd suffered together. I learned about a miscarried child Charlotte lost when she was pregnant, who died when Henry kicked her in the stomach.

"I thought she was cheating on me. She'd been around this old boy a lot, and she was always around Wayne. That's about the time I found out about what they'd been up to, and I got mad and kicked her. I didn't mean to hurt that little one. I would never hurt no baby. I was with you a lot when you were young. Me and your aunt Charlotte would be around your momma and daddy all the time, go honky-tonking together, you know. I would never hurt no little baby."

Charlotte's face lit up for the first time, like she was happy about something. She smiled at me and said, "Yeah. He kicked me right here"—she motioned to her stomach—"and killed my baby." When I asked her why she stayed, she gave me some twisted reason based on a perverse definition of love I didn't understand. "I loved him," she said. "You don't leave the ones you love."

My spirit was heavy. This was my family; the blood I shared with them linked me to this group of vagabonds. I wasn't hateful toward either one of them, nor did I feel animosity. I felt mourning in my spirit for the lives they missed out on because of negative decisions they had made. Henry's felonies were all violent offenses. He killed a man with a shotgun in a bar fight and cut his son-in-law's stomach open with a knife. He shared, "I split him from his belly button to his breast plate. He tried to take me in my own home, and I couldn't let that happen, so I cut him."

The conversation began to wind down. I don't think I could have handled much more emotionally, so I decided to ask a final question before I left.

"Uncle Henry, now that you're older and don't have much time left, do you have any regrets?"

"Yeah, I regret killing that man. I see him every night. He comes and talks to me and reminds me of what I did to him. Scares me pretty bad."

I sat there in silence, not knowing how to respond. Then I looked up and asked another.

"If you could go back, what would you do differently?"

He returned the silence, appearing to ponder the question I'd just thrown at him. It seemed like a useless question to waste much time rolling over, but it was an important one. I truly believe the best teacher is the regret of others. He dropped his head unexpectedly and began to sob.

Charlotte's face withered within her skin. "Stop crying, you titty baby." I sat upright and patted him on the back.

"No. No. It's all right, Uncle Henry," I told him. "You can cry. You should cry. It's been a painful life. You should cry."

"I would be nicer to people. I just wouldn't be so hateful toward anyone and wouldn't want to do anyone no harm. I would just be nicer."

I watched him sob for a life he had missed, memories he wished he could erase, and a future tormented with the mistakes of the past. It's been said that in life people have to lie in the bed they make. I believe that. But lying in that bed is not so we can rest but so that we can be made into ourselves.

Some beds are labored over so intensively they are left fitted and tight, following a militant model of bed making. Self-discipline, self-control, and rule following dominate the lives of people who lie in these types of beds. They are held up as pillars of society, strong and steady. Others are soft, a bit ruffled, and comfortable. They get lots of wear and tear, absorbing jumps, tosses, and tussles. There are always lots of people who visit these kinds of beds. Friends sit for afternoon talks. Children climb for morning snuggles. The need for relationships, expression, and community are rampant in these lives, and these people are seen as friends and companions, trusted and valued.

But some beds are lumpy, broken, squeaky, and hard. They've been left unkempt for years at a time. The sheets are rarely washed, and the mattress has far outlived its firmness. These beds never render a quality night's rest, just enough sleep to get through another day. Most of the time, these people are exhausted when they return home, dropping their lifeless bodies onto these unmade beds, just grateful for a place to lie for a while. In society, we see these people as failures. They can't pay their bills on time. They're usually dirty, with old ragged clothes and cars that sputter on, coughing and wheezing as far as they can for as long as they can.

I used to believe we were all responsible for making our own beds. It was one of the many formulas and instructional guides I used to define life in a more linear way. It seemed simple enough; you make your bed tight and crisp, or you leave it a mess and dirty. Whatever you choose, you have to live with the results. You had to lie in that bed. It was a nice, clean formula.

Meeting my uncle Henry changed that belief for me. We do lie in the beds we make, but so do our children, our wives, our husbands, our brothers, and our sisters. What about them? What about the fact that sometimes we all have to lie in beds we don't make? What about the reality that we have to learn to make beds, and some of us have better teachers than others? What if my mother learned to make her bed from a father who didn't know how to make beds? And what if I learned to make my bed from a mother who didn't know how to make beds?

Sure, somewhere along the winding roads of life, we all have opportunities to make our own beds, but what if by that time it's too late to change the bed we lie in? Before we know it, we are standing at the doorway to the other side, staring death in the eye and seeing for the first time that maybe the bed we slept in our entire lives wasn't really our own but the bed of social, religious, and generational influences. I know that goes against modern-day philosophical and psychological babble, but just maybe there is a bit of nurturing in life that affects the nature of life.

Don't get me wrong; I believe in personal responsibility and being accountable for the decisions we make and don't make in life. I'm just saying that I'm tired of the judgments that go along with circumstances that don't measure up to the accepted norm and, let's face it, that some people have a harder go at it than others. The "pull yourself up by the bootstraps" mentality has become a badge of courage in our society. I wear it as proudly as anyone, but we have allowed it to callous us to the plight of human beings who struggle for their very existence in this country.

I watched as my uncle cried, and I was overwhelmed with the guilt of judgment. In my mind I saw my nicely made bed with ornate pillars and a hanging canopy on one side and his dirty, disheveled tangle of sheets loosely scattered on a rotting cot on the other, and I thought I was better than him. I silently despised his weakness and shamefully harbored an internal pride: "Look what I've overcome." I watched him weep over his bed, the bed his wife had chosen to share with him, and saw the realization on his face that his bed could've been different. That one simple fold of the sheet or arrangement of the mattress could have changed his bed enough to give him a better life than the one he had.

It was a look of hope that crossed his face, and in that instant I realized that Uncle Henry had been made. He was looking at his life and was broken, and I can't help but think in that moment, *That is what life is about. It's about being awed by our own existence. It's about recognizing that this thing called life is bigger than we can imagine, and when all is said and done, the least of us live by the same grace as the highest of us. And yes, we reap what we sow, and the decisions we make do create an effect on the life we live, but we also reap what others sow into us.*

We are both the farmer and the soil; we sow into ourselves and are available to be sown in to. We plant and are planted in. We give and we take, and in the end, each one of us bears beautiful fruit and each one of us has weeds that need to be pulled and each one of us bears responsibility for half our fruit and half the discarded weeds. I believe the amount of fruit one has the ability to reap is in direct proportion to the fruit that is sown. Likewise, the number of weeds reaped is also in direct proportion to the number of weeds sown.

Sixteen

NO BETTER, NO WORSE

*The law, in its majestic equality, forbids the rich
as well as the poor from sleeping under bridges,
begging in the streets, and stealing bread.*

—ANATOLE FRANCE

The flight attendant jarred me with a loud-pitched, "Sir. Sir. Would you like dinner this evening?" and I awoke startled from sleepless dreams.

"No. Thank you."

Only an hour in the air had passed, but it was enough time to sweep through my encounter with Uncle Henry. My visit with him cleared up a lot of questions in my own mind. It wasn't the starting point I'd hoped for but perhaps the one I needed.

It's a funny thing, this thing called life. I've spent so much time thinking about how bad things were for me, how hard it was growing up, and how unfair life can be that I seemed to have missed the blessings I have and the breaks I caught. True, there were some difficult things to deal with, but it could have been much worse, couldn't it? I mean, I could have been born in Henry's lifetime, in a backwoods town with no law, no boundaries, and no one healthy enough to intercede on my behalf. I've failed to see exactly how important my environment has been in shaping who I am and what I've done.

The truth is I had an escape. It began with my mother, who was strong enough to leave my father in the midst of fear for her life. Fear for our lives. I had good grandparents, who although poor were very loving and caring individuals. They did everything they could to give me an exceptional life. I had a man like Papa Cisco, my mom's stepfather, to model to me what a hardworking, faithful man looks like. They gave me opportunities Henry and my dad never got.

I also had the opportunity to interact with a more civilized, educated community as a result of going to college. Attending college brought me into contact with self-reflecting people who valued education. Where Henry and Dad grew up, a man was respected for three things: drinking, fighting, and sleeping with women. Even living in Houston, a large city, brought an entirely different spectrum of values into my life. It is a city that appreciates the arts—music, literature, sculpting, theater, and painting. It is a city, for the most part, that respects human beings—culture, language, and ethnicity. Education was valued there far more than at home. For Henry and Dad, education only got in the way of work. It was a barrier to freedom, individuality, and independence.

It was through education that I have had the greatest advantages. I attended quality schools, more than my share, and interacted with loving and caring adults who gave to me and called from me more than I would have known back home. These encounters began to have a deep impact on what I had the capacity to become.

Don't get me wrong; for the longest time, I didn't take advantage of any of these things, mainly because I didn't believe in them. I was always under the impression that peace, love, happiness, integrity, character, and genuine compassion and selflessness were found only in movies or books. I waited for these things to be revealed as deceptions, just as everything else in my life had been. I looked for what was wrong with the world instead of celebrating what was right with it.

In fact, when things went well was when I was most afraid, for two reasons. Number one, I was waiting for it to end. I was taught early in my life that all good things end. Most of the time, they don't come to an end; they just end. Second, I was scared I would somehow screw it up. I never believed I deserved good things to happen to me or if they did that I would be able to sustain them. I can't tell you how many opportunities I've self-sabotaged because of my fear of blowing them!

No, Henry was the right place for me to start because before meeting Henry I thought I was better than my father. I left Uncle Henry with an understanding that it was just easier for me.

Seventeen

LITTLE GIRLS CHANGE EVERYTHING

She is my joy and heart's delight.

—ROBERT WEVER

The plane ride so far had been everything I'd hoped it would be. I was afraid I'd forget all the information my uncles had given me. I knew these stories would most likely be lost if I didn't capture them, and so the fact that they came back so easily was pleasantly surprising. I laid my head back and thought about the next uncle I'd met.

"Hi, Uncle Jared. You're a hard man to find. Do you know you're listed under the wrong last name in the phone book? I would have never been able to find you if Henry hadn't given me some information first."

His voice was gravelly as he spoke. "Yeah, I know. Had trouble with the law some time ago. Just trying to stay clean; don't want to be bothered by no one."

"Oh, OK. I understand. I'm just trying to find my dad and wanting to meet any of the family I can come into contact with. Have you heard from or seen him in a while?"

"No. Ain't no one heard from Stan in over twenty years from what I understand. He's just fallen off the planet. Leones do that, you know."

"I'm learning that pretty quickly. Listen, I do a lot of work in Florida, and I have a trip coming up in a couple of weeks. I'd like to meet you and your family if you're open to it."

"I don't see why not. It'd be nice to see one of Stan's boys. I ain't seen Stan since he was a boy. I got locked up for a long time when he was just, let's see, well, fourteen, I guess. Ain't seen him since then."

"Well, I haven't seen him since I was 5," I said, "and Henry is the only one of you guys I've been able to actually meet."

"We'd love to meet you, Stanley. Give me a call when you get here, and we can go from there."

It was with eager anticipation and great reserve that I set out to meet Uncle Jared. The drive from West Palm Beach was about three hours, and the thoughts of what I would find in this man probed at my heart every minute of the drive.

His home was nicer than I expected, a true contrast to Uncle Henry's. Whatever Jared's mistakes from the past were, it appeared, at least on the surface he'd been able to overcome them and make something of himself. Relief suddenly flowed through me as I glanced around and took note of the surrounding neighborhood. Although I didn't have as much anxiety about meeting Jared, I have to say I was comforted by knowing we were within shouting distance of other people.

Four bedrooms and three baths. Compared to Henry's, Uncle Jared's house was a mansion, and by all other accounts, it looked nice as well. I was greeted by my cousins, thirteen-year-old Jeanette and nineteen-year-old Jackie. They were very warm and inviting and curiously young considering Jared was their father. He was seventy-two years old! Apparently, he took after his father, Grandpa Walter, who had children well into his sixties. Being unable to have children of my own because of hormonal disadvantages, I admit I was a little envious. OK. I was a lot envious.

Aunt Michelle was an average looking woman, with large glasses. She had the sweetest personality, wore clothes that were thoughtfully selected and was very likeable. Uncle Jared stood about the same height as Aunt Michelle, approximately 5'7" tall, and he was built like a truck. Squatty, with broad shoulders and biceps that bulged like a 21 year-old, it was evident he'd been in very good shape at one time.

His head was full of hair, an attractive gray-white blend, thick and bushy with Elvis-like sideburns. A spongy nose, strong jawline and chin, and bright twinkling eyes gave him the look of an intelligent Mafioso. We stepped into the spacious living room, obviously decorated with care, and sat on the couches, myself between the two girls and Uncle Jared and Aunt Michelle opposite us.

"Thank you guys for making the time for me to visit."

Jared spoke up, the definite leader and spokesperson for the family. "Not a problem. There's not much else going on around here very often, and besides that, I never thought I would meet one of my brother's kids. I haven't seen your daddy since he was a boy."

"He wasn't a big part of my life either," I replied.

"I remember him though. I liked him. He was a good guy, even back then."

"That's what they tell me," I agreed. "My memories of him aren't so good. That's why I'm trying to find him." Uncle Jared seemed to stiffen a bit. "Not that I want to get back at him or anything, just want some different memories...that's all."

"Well, people change. Time tends to do that to you. You get old, and it's like you start to slow down and not do the things you used to do."

He was thoughtful and reflective, and I responded with my awareness of his good fortune. "Well, it looks like you did well for yourself."

"Yeah, I've done good. Changed a lot. I own this house, you know. Don't have to pay nobody nothing for this place. It's mine, bought it outright."

"It's a nice place. I can't believe how big it is!"

"Yeah, lot of room. Four bedrooms and three baths. Girls have their own rooms, and we have a spare now that JoAnn moved out into her own place."

"It's real nice."

We went on like this for a couple of hours or so, every statement I made was with an effort to build some sort of relationship with him, and every response from his words seemed calculated and careful. As the time passed and they began to trust me, I noticed the responses became more and more revealing. They offered me something to drink, I accepted, and as Jared began to share more personal information, so accordingly, I started to ask more personal questions.

Although Jared began to talk more and was actually pretty chatty, he never really got into any details about what life was like for him growing up. Every time I broached the subject, he got quiet, waited a second or two to roll the question over, and gave minimal information in his responses.

"What was life like for you growing up?" I asked.

"It wasn't too bad. Normal life, I guess you'd say. Momma was home, and Daddy did his thing," Uncle Jared responded.

"I heard he was a bootlegger. They said he used to make white lightning?"

"Yeah, Daddy made him some drink, would sell some to the men in town."

I longed to know him through Jared's experiences. "What was he like?" I asked.

"He was a good man."

"I heard he was hard on y'all."

"No. I wouldn't say he was hard on us. He just didn't take no crap, and he'd get into your butt if you weren't doing what you were supposed to be doing."

We went on and on like this for hours. He would respond more thoroughly when I asked about what he did for a living, how he met his wife, how did he like having all girls, and so on. It was only when I got to the more meaningful questions where painful memories seemed to not allow him to speak as freely that I sensed a subtle yet certain shift in his responses. I was certainly enjoying his company. He was funny in a Fred Sanford sort of way.

He definitely struck me as the kind of man other men would want to be around. There were admirable, leadership-type qualities in him, and I could sense them just through the conversation. But I didn't travel to Florida for small talk. I traveled to learn more about the truth of my family, and I was getting a bit frustrated. I decided to try a more direct approach.

"What were you locked up for?" I questioned.

"I've been out for some time now, and no trouble. The grandmother of a li'l ole girl I was dating got upset because I kept her out all night. We didn't go all the way, but…"

I sat there as Uncle Jared told me an elaborate story of the excitement of youth, alcohol, parties, sex, lies, and deceit. None of which was true according to Henry. Maybe it was because his family was there. I would certainly change the truth to make myself look better in front of my children if I had been accused of the sorts of things he was accused of. Maybe he was telling the truth. I'm just not certain.

When I'd spent time with Uncle Henry he'd been very open about everything I'd asked. When I asked him specifically about Uncle Jared the conversation was both illuminating and tragic. It seems Jared was arrested and charged with raping and molesting two little girls, the daughters of a woman he was dating. He was originally sentenced to life in prison without the chance of parole. I was surprised to hear such a harsh sentence was delivered and felt a little proud of the court system. I have absolutely no tolerance for rapists and child molesters, having been raped at twelve by an uncle myself. But this was in the 1950s, and back then the sentences were more comparable to the crime, and from the victim's perspective, I think they got it right.

He served 25 years and was later released from prison after his case was reevaluated and the sentence was deemed too harsh. As a result, Jared could never leave the state of Florida, confined to the swampy surroundings by a lifetime parole consequence of his actions. He was a young man when he made his mistake, and it cost him a lot of his life. I don't believe he was completely honest with me about what got him into prison, but I was fascinated to learn what he did while he spent his time there.

"This might be a stupid question, but what was it like for you?"

"Well, it wasn't good, but I made good out of it. I made the choice to 'do what was asked,' so they was kind of lenient on me, you know. I got to do things with limited supervision, and that gave me some freedom the other inmates didn't have."

I wanted to know more about what his choices included and what he valued, so I asked, "Tell me one thing you did in there that was good."

"I was a boxer, undefeated. I got a ring and everything because I was the prison champion. Back then we didn't have no weight classes or nothing; just anybody fought anybody, and the winner was the winner. I was lean, you know; 165 pounds is all I weighed."

"And you fought anyone?"

"Oh yeah. Anyone. I never backed down from no one. Lot of times they was bigger than me, and they would pound on me a bit, but like I said, I was undefeated. Some of them were 185 pounds, and some of them were 225 pounds. It didn't matter much to me."

I reflected on the values my dad and his family grew up with and where it took them. In a "live by the sword, die by the sword" environment like theirs, brute force and violence were the pinnacle of admiration, and there were none tougher nor more violent than them. But the rewards of anger and a quick temper, selfishness, and an offensive disposition are summed up in the struggles of a difficult life.

The stuff of a good life consists of those qualities that describe great men throughout history. A mild temperament, careful consideration and decisiveness; unconcerned with the opinions of others; a love of perseverance and hard work; a readiness to listen open mindedly; uncompromising integrity; and wisdom derived from life experiences...and humility.

I cleared my mind of my own opinions and celebrated an accomplishment for him. "Wow, and you won all your fights?"

"Every one of them."

"How did you do it?"

"I would rest my head right here." He leaned forward and jabbed his hand into my chest, right below the throat. "And I'd just keep coming, punching in every angle I could. I was real fast and strong too." He smiled and flexed his seventy-two-year-old biceps, which were still as hard as concrete. I bet he could still whoop a few people if he had to. "I always told myself, 'You're a Leone, Jared. There ain't no quit in Leones. There ain't no quit *at all* in Leones.'

"I never quit and never got knocked out. I got knocked around a time or two, but I'd just shake it off and keep coming straight ahead. I was the champion until I was released." He reached up and received something from Jeanette and then turned around and handed it to me. It was a solid-gold boxing championship ring. The prison name was labeled on it, alongside his. It wasn't a Super Bowl ring with all the honors an athlete would derive from the championship. But it was an acknowledgment of a given skill, and worthy of celebration. I was proud for him.

"So that got you a reputation then. I bet no one messed with you after they saw you fight."

"They pretty much left me alone, and I left them alone. Just minded my business and did my time. It wasn't like it is today, all these gangs and crazy stuff. You didn't have to worry about gangs and joining something to survive. Back then, a man could stand on his own."

"What about when you first went in? Did anyone try to mess with you then?"

He sat there in silence for a moment, and I knew this was a question he needed to think about before he responded. Rather than talking through the silence, I sat with him, embracing the quiet and patiently waiting for his reply. "Yeah. There was a man, a black man, when I got in there, said he knowed what I did and he was gone pay me back for it. He waited until wash time when he tried something, but I was ready for it.

"He'd been talking shit to everybody that would listen, telling them I was a 'Chester' and he was gone pay me back at shower time. I got a little ole shank, like a knife I made out of a piece of fence, and I kept it in my towel. I was walking to the shower, and he was standing there whistling at me, telling me how pretty I looked. I looked right at him and told him if he wanted to sample, then come on…and he did. He was a big ole boy, and I knew I had to put a stop to what he was saying right there. He had to be an example for him and the others."

"So you stabbed him?"

"When people call you a Chester in prison, then everybody wants to get after you 'cause they think you hurt little kids. This girl I was locked up for was not much younger than me, only 5 years, but because of the sentence brought by the court, they all think it's the little ones, so I had to make an example of him quick, or my time could have been real hard. He came at me, and right before he reached up to grab me, I pulled that shank out my towel and shoved it in his stomach about nine or ten times. He fell right there. Everyone went on with their business, so I walked over and finished showering, then went on back to my cell.

"The guards found him like that, crumpled up on the floor. Blood was running from him to the drain. I never wanted to kill no man, but I'll admit it; I did what I had to do with him. No one ever informed the guards that it was me either. I figured, maybe the guards were glad he was dead. One less troublemaker to deal with."

I was silent. two uncles, two murderers. What a family legacy.

"I got an education in there too. I liked to cook, and they had all kinds of classes in there, so I took some culinary courses and became a certified chef. I even got my high-school GED in there. I believe I was the first in the family to have a high-school education; didn't none of the Leones go to school. We Leones just didn't have time for education."

"Wait a minute. You were a boxing champion, a certified chef, and you got your GED. Prison wasn't all bad for you then?"

"It is what you make it. I decided since I was stuck in there, I might as well make the most of it. I didn't have much trouble to worry about, maybe a new guy every now and then who wanted to make a name for himself, take out the champ, but I put that to rest pretty quick if it came up. After the shower incident, people knew I wasn't nobody's bitch, so they let me be."

116

"Did you ever think about what you did while you were in there?" I asked.

"All I did was think. Lots of time for it. I thought about the mistakes I made a lot. Wished I would have done something different. I was so young and didn't know any better, but prison taught me different."

"Did you ever think about getting out?" My mind thought about shows like *Breakout* and *Prison Break* and others. The finality of being locked up for such a long time would have naturally led to a creative mind trying to figure a way out.

"All the time. I prayed a lot too. I said, 'God, if you get me out of here, I'll go the straight path.' You see, I wasn't supposed to never get out. They locked me up for life because of a conspiracy the arresting officer set up against me. They knew I didn't do anything wrong, but I'd had some trouble with him before and he set me up real bad. I didn't think I was gone ever get out, but I prayed. I decided if I got out, I would go the straight path. I been out over twenty years and ain't never been in trouble again."

"What was the biggest thing you changed when you got out?"

"I quit all that drinking and honky-tonking."

"You quit drinking? What drove you to do that?"

He looked at his wife, Michelle, and smiled at her. "Your aunt did. I was drinking quite a bit, and I got real mean with her a few times. She got pregnant with my oldest, JoAnn, and said I had to choose: the alcohol or her and the girls. She's a real good woman. Real strong, and I didn't want to lose my girls, so I just stopped drinking and ain't never been in no more trouble."

"So, if you had to sum up your life in one sentence—what you've been through, where you came from, what you've learned—what would you say?"

"Little girls change everything," he replied softly.

Eighteen

TURBULENT REFLECTIONS

*You and I have need of the strongest spell that can be found
to wake us from the evil enchantment of worldliness.*

—C. S. LEWIS

I jolted awake, startled by the rocking back and forth of the plane. The fasten-seatbelt sign was illuminated, and the flight attendant made the announcement about temporary turbulence again. I pulled the window shade up and peered at the endless sea of cloudy sky. It really is an amazing thing to see the earth from the window of a plane. There is a meditative quality when you're soaring at 24,000 feet in the air. No stoplights. No ambulances, police cars, fire trucks. No honking horns, screeching cars, or angry pedestrians, not on a good flight anyway.

Yet beneath the clouds, life is still happening. People still experience joy and pain. Relationships are won and lost, and tragedy still happens every moment of every day. My journey up until that point had taught me a lot about my family and myself. I'd been told my entire life that I was evil, that evil flowed through my veins. I had in my head memories of evil men, and I made them out to be monsters. Having met a couple of my uncles, I realized that those thoughts were just not true. Each one of them had made mistakes, but in each one I found a certain goodness that I recognize in myself, buried deep within them. They were kind and grateful, hospitable and genuine, and I enjoyed being around them. They weren't monsters and part of me felt relief. If they weren't monsters, then I wasn't either.

People do the best they can with what they know, even if what they know is poverty, or survival. There is a truth in each of us, and that truth declares that we are real; that we are people who make mistakes and who stumble around in our own imperfections, trying to figure it all out. I love the picture Margery Williams paints in *The Velveteen Rabbit*. It is the most beautiful picture of our "real" identity I have ever come across:

"What is REAL?" asked the Rabbit one day, when they were lying side by side near the nursery fender, before Nana came to tidy the room. "Does it mean having things that buzz inside you and a stick-out handle?"

"Real isn't how you are made," said the Skin Horse. "It's a thing that happens to you. When a child loves you for a long, long time not just to play with, but REALLY loves you, then you become Real."

"Does it hurt?"

"Sometimes," said the Skin Horse, for he was always truthful. "When you are Real you don't mind being hurt."

"Does it happen all at once," he asked, "or bit by bit?"

"It doesn't happen all at once," said the Skin Horse. "You become. It takes a long time. That's why it doesn't happen to people who break easily, or who have sharp edges or have to be carefully kept. Generally, by the time you are Real, most of your hair has been loved off, and your eyes drop out and you get loose in the joints and very shabby. But those things don't matter at all, because once you are Real you can't be ugly, except to people who don't understand."

Stanley Leone Jr.

I'm not angry with my uncles, and I don't hate them for what they did, are doing, and will do. In fact, I love them for what they are. I love the truth that binds us together in life. I see two men who were deceived into believing they were less than they are. two men who were blinded by the hurt inflicted on them through their environments and responded with vengeance, inflicting pain on those around them. I see two men who became so lost in the lies of poverty that they did not find the peace that comes with focusing on what matters most in life: loving relationships, and empathy for ourselves and others.

I try to look beyond behavior to see the context in which those behaviors are acted out. It is too easy to just hate people for what they do. It's too easy to feel superior to people who make mistakes. In my own life, I have done just as many hurtful, shameful deeds as either one of my uncles. I could have been arrested several times for crimes I had committed, many more times than the single felony from high school. I have hurt people. I have lied. I have stolen. I have been as guilty as anyone else when it comes to making mistakes.

Yet I consider myself a good man. I am nothing more and nothing less than a human being living with flaws, trying to do the best I can. I no longer have the desire to judge my uncles, or my father for that matter. Because I'd been told that I was a bad person simply because of who my family was, I'd spent my life trying to prove I was better than them. When I began this journey, I didn't realize it, but I'd already made my judgments; too willing to condemn them as bad people and myself as a good person.

I'm not saying we should be indifferent to the behaviors of others. That would be to say something entirely different. Indifference is not the same as being nonjudgmental. I guess I'm saying that none of us are without fault, and so we should offer grace and forgiveness when people make mistakes. I think I have done well with my life given where I started, but I didn't have the same kind of life Jared and Henry had. They had different pains, different insecurities, and who knows? Maybe I wouldn't have done as well as they did if I'd been given their circumstances.

They inherited many of the challenges they faced from their father, in the same way my father passed down his sins. For many years my behaviors were shaped and molded by the standards my dad had set before me. It wasn't until other healthy and appropriate adults entered my life that I was able to begin the process of changing my behaviors. When my father was the only example I had, I did what he did. When I encountered other men and women who behaved differently, people I could respect, who didn't hurt me, I began to do what they did, and more times than not, it was better. I wasn't drawn to people who were worse than the people already in my life. I was always drawn to people who could offer me a better way of doing things.

I think, as I sat there waiting to see the man I had hated for 25 years, I was beginning to realize that I had no right to hatred. This realization didn't come out of a desire to be a forgiving guy. It came out of a broken heart. Out of the fact that I am so aware of my own faults. My own anger. The violence I have committed. My broken heart is a result of truly seeing that the grace I so desperately depend on is the same grace I have so adamantly denied my family.

I didn't expect to learn so much about myself on this journey. More than anything I think I have a newfound gratefulness for my life, my family, and the circumstances I've been through. None of it was perfect, obviously, but it was ultimately effective enough to get me to where I am at this moment in my life. For the most part, I like where I'm at and I like who I am. I realized through my visitations that it's very easy for me to take a negative approach to what I've experienced because it was hard to live through. I wasn't aware of just how negative I'd become, and I'd been unable to see the value in the people from my past.

What if Uncle Jared and Uncle Henry came from good families? What if Grandma Alice tucked them in at night, read bedtime stories, kissed them on the cheeks, told them she loved them, and prayed out loud over them, beseeching God to bless them with favor and protect them from evil? What if she professed out loud their greatness and uniqueness, how special they were, how incredibly precious they were?

What if Grandpa Walter played baseball with them, took them mountain climbing and camping, wrestled with them in loving ways, and told them he loved them and was proud of the men they were? I can't help but think if they'd grown up in this type of environment that their lives and the lives of all those who are connected to them wouldn't have turned out differently. What if they grew up with the balance of consistent love and boundaries? They would have been different men—real men.

What if my own life had been different? What if I'd felt loved? What if I'd felt wanted? What if I'd felt valued and appreciated? What if I'd been protected rather than taken advantage of? What if I'd felt like I was the most precious boy on the face of this planet? What if I'd felt like my parents would miss me if I died? What if I'd felt like I had what it took to be good enough.

These are the questions we all ask at one time or another, and only those with the most abundant lives—lives filled with people who already know how to live and love well—can ever arrive at truthful answers to those questions. It's not money that answers them. It's not possessions. It's people. Relationships that mean something. It's how we're loved and how we love in return that can make a difference in who we are and how we act.

Nineteen

Within Prison Walls

*I think in the case of horror, it's a chance to confront
a lot of your worse fears and those fears usually have
to do, ironically, with powerlessness and isolation.*

—Adam Arkin

Of all the trips I made, Uncle Wayne was the one I was most nervous about. I had to get approval through an extensive background check by the prison to visit. When he walked out he was securely chained and spoke to me from behind six-inch-thick bulletproof glass. All of that was enough to make a person nervous in itself, but what made me the most hesitant was that Wayne was, by all accounts, the closest person to my father.

Wayne and my dad were only a couple of years apart in age. Given the closeness of their age and given that my younger brother and I are only separated by eleven months, I understood the bond between them. I knew, of the brothers I would have the opportunity to meet, Wayne knew my dad the best. If anyone could give me dependable information about him, it was Wayne.

It didn't help either that no one seemed to like Wayne, and no doubt for some good reasons. Henry seemed to spit his name out when he referred to him, and apparently it was Wayne whom Henry was trying to kill when he shot my dad in the leg. Because Jared was so young when he was put in prison, he didn't know Wayne all that well, but what he did know about him—the drugs and beating on women—he didn't like.

My mother and the rest of her side of the family didn't have many good things to say about him either. Mom told me that Wayne was the worse of them all, and Stan got in most of his trouble defending Wayne when he started trouble at bars. I heard stories of him raping women in bars as they went into restrooms. He would follow them back, drag them into a stall, and assault them. My mother remembered men coming more than one time to the apartments we lived in when I was a child, looking for Wayne. My dad always got involved in cleaning up his messes.

He was also the drug addict of the family, although all of them dipped their hands into a drug or two every now and then. Crack was his Achilles's heel, and it was that addiction that got him into prison for the rest of his life. My mom's brother, Uncle Robert, told me of the destructive tendencies of my uncle Wayne. He told me of him beating a young girl he was with until she was black and blue because she simply *looked at* my dad. Wayne expected her to keep her head down the entire time, which she did for the most part, but when she looked up to acknowledge something my father said, Wayne went into a frenzy.

The next morning Wayne called Uncle Robert and my dad and told them he needed their help. When they arrived at his apartment, that poor girl was hung up on the ceiling, standing on a chair in the middle of the room, with a series of tied-up belts looped around her neck.

Her face was bloody and cheeks stained with a night full of fear and tears. She had been standing there without sleep while Wayne taunted her. When they arrived at his apartment, he said he needed their advice because he'd been sitting there all night trying to decide what to do with her. He said he couldn't make up his mind. Dad slapped the hell out of him and let the young girl down.

He was the man who got me high as a 5-year-old, blowing smoke in my face and making bets about which way I would stumble. The worse part of it is they all say he's the softest of the bunch, never fighting his own fights but hiding behind my father for protection. Henry told me Wayne never went into a fight without a weapon because he had no confidence in his hands.

I guess it's a kind of miracle I even had the opportunity to see Uncle Wayne. Henry gave me his contact information, but with two counts of homicide and one count of rape, in Texas, I wasn't even sure if he'd still be there. Texas isn't lenient when it comes to murderers.

As I pulled off the main highway into the James Allred Maximum Security Penitentiary, I felt anxious and tense. The property was massive, surrounded with barbwire fencing, towers positioned at intervals among the different housing units, and a security check station. I was asked to turn the engine off, pop the hood, open the trunk, and step out of the car.

They spent quite a bit of time searching my vehicle and examining my license and had me sign a sheet of paper next to my uncle's number. That was the first thing I noticed. No one cared about his name. His life was reduced to a number.

The drive into the prison was eerie. The concrete driveway seemed to wind back and forth like a serpent cutting through the hide of green pastures. After having my car searched and examined, my ID checked and validated, I was allowed to proceed to the parking lot where I was to leave my vehicle.

I pulled into a space in the back, lowered my head on the steering wheel, and cried. *Why are you doing this to yourself, Stanley? You don't have to do this. You can just pull out and leave now. You've met Henry and Jared, seen that they're not monsters. There's no reason to continue putting yourself through this.* But I didn't drive away.

I didn't know what I was feeling. Sadness, nervousness, anger, hatred...love, and remorse. All of them hit me at once, and I didn't know how to handle it. It's not that I was unfamiliar with being afraid. I've been afraid most my life.

I was afraid of my father. Then I was afraid of my mother. I was afraid of being homeless, of not having food to eat, of not being able to protect my younger brothers and sister. I was afraid when I woke up and found that my older brother had disappeared. It would be six years before I found out what happened to him. I was afraid of being laughed at, not being good enough, not fitting in, of failure. I would in no way ever brag about this, but I've had this bad habit as long as I can remember of not running away from the things I was afraid of. I usually ran right at them, face first, and that's what I did with Uncle Wayne.

I stepped out of the car and prepared myself for the worst. My walk had a little more swag to it. My body tensed. My eyes scanned this way and that way, taking in everything around me, analyzing my surroundings. I convinced myself right there, if I was going to meet a monster, he wouldn't see the fear I felt. I prepared physically as well as mentally and emotionally for the encounter at hand.

I walked into the first building and had to remove everything from my pockets, my shoes, jewelry, and belt, only to be told I had to go back to my car to leave my hat, my uncle's letter, business cards, and paper money, as nothing but my keys, ID, and a ten-dollar roll of quarters were allowed into the facility.

I returned and went through the same process again, then gave my uncle's number to the lady behind glass, and waited for the first door to slide open. I walked through it and came immediately to another security door that had to be buzzed by the same lady before it would open.

I was shocked by how homey the place felt as I stepped through two glass doors. There was a painting of who I assumed to be the warden hanging on the wall directly in front of the entrance doors. He sat there greeting each visitor with a "welcome to my home" smile. There was a check-in counter immediately to the right, and a sweet, grandmotherly lady sat behind the desk signing people in as they entered. She did not seem to fit. When I approached her, I half expected her to offer me a piece of apple pie and ask me to have a seat to chat a while.

There was no apple pie, and I didn't get offered a seat. I signed in as a guest of number such and such and then directed toward a security booth with two stainless-steel doors in place. I realized this was the part of the prison only meant for the families and friends of the prisoners, never to be breeched by the prisoners who resided in the actual prison itself.

I checked in again at another security booth and was waved through the first set of stainless-steel doors. There was a buzzing—the doors being unlocked from behind the bulletproof glass in the security booth—and I was standing in a small, open transition point with another set of stainless-steel doors in front of me. Those doors were also engaged with a buzzing sound, and after looking back to get the OK from the security guard, I stepped through them as well.

Twenty

LITTLE BOYS AND PRISONS

That's what it takes to be a hero, a little gem of innocence inside you that makes you want to believe that there still exists a right and wrong, that decency will somehow triumph in the end.

—LISE HAND

When I got onto the actual property of the prison and began making my way through the grounds, the sidewalk cut through a massive courtyard. It was quite surreal but beautiful, with flowers decorating each side of the sidewalk for about one hundred yards. It was the perfect reminder for those who were locked up of what they'd lost. It was a picture of the beauty of a life they could no longer participate in.

There were three housing units on either side of the main building directly in the middle of the property. There was a prisoner working the flowers, and I felt myself go emotionally numb, remembering where I was, and there was no more emotion. No more fear.

The day was beautiful, with the sun shining down and a cool wind hitting me in the face. It was so easy to breathe in the open air of the courtyard, and at any moment a person could lose himself or herself in the contradictions of that place. On the surface the place had the feel of a park until one saw inmates walking around in their jumpsuits. The guards didn't have to torture, manhandle, or threaten the prisoners to make them realize what they'd lost with the decisions they'd made in lives gone wrong. Mother Nature inflicted far more than any man could with its constant reminder of the beauty in the world.

The brilliance of the sun; the glory of a soft, cloudy sky speckled with every shade of blue imaginable; the peacefulness of a cool, crisp wind dancing smoothly through your hair and kissing you softly on the neck. Subtle reminders that you are no longer free and no longer able to participate in a remarkable world. The smell of fresh-cut grass. The chirping of crickets leaping from blade to blade, playing carefree in the thickness of a lush lawn, chasing one another like innocent children playing tag on a playground. To never be able to experience the beauty and gift of nature freely and openly would be the worst prison of all.

A woman and child were leaving as I entered the doors for the main building, and I got caught looking at the boy, wondering how he was feeling. Wondering if he thought prison was normal, having to visit his daddy behind bars.

The child was smiling, playfully skipping around, excited to hold the door open for what I believed to be his mother. She seemed bitter but very courteous as I helped the boy hold the door open. I thought about her too. What was her life like? How would she raise that happy little boy on her own, and still, how would she keep him happy and free from repeating the patterns of his father? When would he arrive at the unhappy step of where I stood, asking similar questions?

I wondered if he would turn out like me. I wondered if there would be someone who would intersect his path and bring a picture of a different reality, one that promised truth and freedom. A life very different from that which he would remember of this place. I wondered if his life held the painful experiences in his future that I went through. Will this woman turn from man to man, jumping in and out of relationships, struggling with intimacy, trust, and the security we all seek, never stopping to consider what affect her aimless, dysfunctional, unhealthy bagging of each man would do to the smile that shined on his face?

Will he know the fear of watching his mother be raped? Will he understand the torment of having his masculinity taken from him, as I did, through emotional or physical abuse like when my uncle raped me? Will he turn to gangs for safety and acceptance? Will he question? I mean, will he really look at himself and question, *Am I good enough? Why am I not worth loving? Do I have what it takes? Am I going to make it?* Will he face the demons that are being birthed in his life as he stands there smiling, holding the door open for strangers to pass through, for strange experiences and painful memories to pass through? Will he be violent? Will he get hurt and then be vengeful, hurting people the way he's been hurt? Where will he end up when all his decisions have been weighed and balanced?

I wondered if he would be like so many of the kids I talk to: angry, hardened, and hopeless as they passed through life. I continued to hold the door with the boy until finally he turned around and glanced up so that he faced me. "Thank you," he said, releasing the door and running off to catch up with his mother.

I stood in that doorway, captivated by the implications of this small child. Watching him walk through that beautiful courtyard seemingly oblivious to the setting couldn't have been any more surreal. A moment for an artist to capture. I turned and stepped inside, and though I was there only for a short period of time, I instantly realized how much brighter the sunlit sky was than the fluorescent lights that illuminated the building.

The entire wall to my left was glass, and I noticed there were round tables set up in a room that looked like a cafeteria, with prisoners and their visitors sitting around them. I didn't know how this would work, but sitting next to Wayne wasn't what I wanted to do. Not because I was afraid of him but because I was afraid of how I might react to him. The last thing I needed was for him to say something stupid about my mom as I probed for answers about the past. My biggest fear was letting the past in any way affect my future, and I decided that I would refuse to give the past that much power over me. I hardened my mind and proceeded with resolve.

It was cold. The air conditioning had to be set in the low sixties. The lady who took my ID had a jacket on. The air had changed too, from an airy breeze to a heavy, thick, wall of oxygen, more like cotton than air. It smelled artificially sterile. Like it had been in a constant state of being wiped down, again and again.

I proceeded to a table just around a corner with a security guard waiting there. She took my paper with my uncle's number and directed me to the back where the segregated units could visit. I was at S-8, and I learned that segregated prisoners were those who were deemed a threat to the rest of the prison population and removed, being placed in isolation for the duration of their stay. I walked through the visitors sitting at their tables, staring at anyone who stared at me, feeling like I needed to muster up as much "Leone bravado" as I could—I simply couldn't look nervous. There before me was a long, closed-off section in the middle of the room.

There were about fourteen seats divided by walls with a phone on each side between the visitor and the inmate. Each person appeared to be sitting in a phone booth, although there wasn't as much privacy because the backs were completely open on both the visitor's side and the inmate side. Both walls were windows, in the front and back, and the prisoners sat in seats that coincided with the seats their visitors were sitting in. But the prisoners had nothing separating them from each other. Able to hear everything that was said, exposed in this long corridor together.

I had a seat next to a lady waiting for her boyfriend, and we talked a while. When she told me she was there to see her boyfriend, she smiled, as if she was proud. I thought, *Why is she smiling about this?* I told her I was there to see my uncle, but I would have to visit with him from behind glass. She said I could have requested a contact visit, one where I could actually touch him, but when I told her he wasn't allowed one, she quickly lit up with an "Ohhhh." The security guard approached me and said I was in the wrong space, that my inmate would be in the back section.

Standing, I thanked the lady for taking the time to talk with me, wished her the best of luck, and hurried to the isolated booths. I waited patiently to interview a man I'd hated as much as I had my father.

Twenty-One

THE BOGEYMAN'S CLOSET

If a man harbors any sort of fear, it percolates
through all his thinking, damages his personality,
makes him a landlord to a ghost.

—LLOYD C. DOUGLAS

At first, I sat to wait for Wayne. Then I stood up. This might sound funny, but for some reason I wanted him to see me at my full stature the first time he laid eyes on me. My legs were a little more than shoulder width apart, my arms folded across my chest, and I kept my chin tilted down, looking out the top of lowered eyebrows, waiting for the locked door to open. I clearly wanted him to see and hear my attitude. I had to be strong, if I wanted his respect.

There was a window in the middle of the door, a foot wide and two feet long. I waited what seemed like an eternity but what was probably close to six or seven minutes, when I saw him approach the door. He looked up for a moment, making eye contact, and lowered his face again as they maneuvered him into the room.

They brought him in shackles. His hands were linked to his feet with a chain that swayed as he walked. The dim light in the room shimmered

133

dully off every inch of steel. The officer lowered, bending at the waist, to unshackle his feet, opened the door, and let him in the room. He then locked the door behind Wayne, who was still handcuffed with his arms behind his back.

Wayne looked at me with a look of recognition, lowered his eyes to the floor, and then squatted down to what they call a "bean hole" to stick his handcuffed hands through. This was how the officers uncuffed him. It took everything in me to not stand up and shout, "What are you doing? Don't unchain him! Are you crazy?" The very thought of letting a man like this loose, even in the closet like the one we were meeting in, was a terrifying prospect. He stood up and rubbed his wrists, staring at me, smirking as if to say, "I knew you'd come."

His hands were still cuffed, but they were free from the shackles that bound them to his feet. Slowly, taking his time, Wayne slipped and scuffled toward the phone on the wall in front of me on his side of the glass. He sat down with a coolness that made me think he was saying everything had been taken care of and he would be out of that place today. He put his hands on the ledge in front of him and looked hard at me, then smiled. I stared back...hard. We each grabbed the phone off the wall. I braced myself for the sound of his voice, like just the sound of it would be an assault.

Those deep, dark-set eyes looked up toward me, and he nodded as if to say "What's up." Those eyes haunted me as I sat on the cold cement bench reserved especially for guests who came to see these isolated prisoners. Each of the inmates around us seemed to look through me and look nowhere at all. There was a blankness about them, and I could see right away that Uncle Wayne was a man lost in his own void. The sad reality was that he did not even realize it. An air about him suggested superiority and authority.

His eyes were telling. A frenzy floated in his irises, filling them like cataracts, looking for some way to ooze out into the room with him. I saw hate and maliciousness. I saw the multiple victims, like the young girl he beat, nearly killing her, the women he raped, the people he killed.

They seemed to dance around in his eyes, waving their hands through the murky fog of the frenzy, like a swimmer treading water. The darkness consumed me as I sat there lost in the thought of this man holding me when I was a child. Angry at the memory of him blowing smoke in my face. This man, who my father trusted and protected, was a real-life boogeyman. He was the monster from childhood stories who lay in wait in closets and hid under beds.

I know it seems like I was judging him, and I'll be honest, I was. I'd had such an incredible experience with my other two uncles and so wanted to approach Wayne the same way, but I couldn't shake the feeling I got from him the moment I was pulled into the gaze of those cold, angry, blazing eyes. I don't think there are evil people in the world. There are people who think they are evil, and those are the ones we have to be cautious of. My uncle was one of those people. He was so lost in the lies he believed about himself that, for him, the lies became truth, and the truth was a lie.

The brilliant, loving, and kind child within him had been imprisoned by the deceitful words of pain and suffering. Somewhere in him that child was lost, alone, and afraid, but unfortunately no candle survived to light the way to his great escape. Short of divine intervention, that child's case would go cold, and the world would never know what happened to him.

He spoke first. "Stanley."

"Yeah," I responded.

"It sure is good to see you. I ain't seen you since you was a boy."

There was an unemotional tone to his words, detached from not only me but the rest of the world altogether. He spoke like he had to remember how.

"You look like your daddy. Built like him too. You work out, huh?"

I replied, "I used to. Just stay in shape now."

For some reason I felt proud. For whatever reason something inside of me wanted this man to respect me. There was a sharp pain in my heart as he repeated what Henry and Jared both told me—I look like my dad.

Breathing was difficult, the air still heavy, and I pulled the mouthpiece of the phone away so he couldn't hear me breathing heavily in the phone. I never looked away. Not sure if I ever blinked.

As I sat there, I was aware of the reality that I would never return to this place, that I would never see or hear from this man again, and I felt a sense of urgency to take in everything about him.

My first thought when I saw him was that he didn't look anything like what I thought he would. He was tall, actually about 6', but he seemed to stand even taller. He was thin, but he carried himself like a solidly built man. His shoulders were broad, like mine, and his chest was broad but not thick.

I thought he definitely had a dominating presence about him. He looked like his father, the infamous Walter from a picture Henry had, the only picture in existence of my grandfather. He was definitely something to look at.

His nose was sort of round, dimpled with blackheads, and spongy. It looked like what I would expect Santa Claus's nose to look like, or the fat guy from *The Sopranos*. His face was not round and dumpy but not long and thin either. He was somewhere in the middle. His eyes were very deep set with dark rings under them. They were black.

He had a heavy brow that made his eyes seem pressed deep into his skull. His lips were thin, and he had a strong chin, squared and flat. His face sloped prominently downward and frown wrinkles hovered over either side of his mouth. Other than that, for a 57-year-old man who lived the life he did, he was relatively wrinkle free. In fact, compared to the other brothers I'd met, he looked pretty good.

His ears were big up top, but he had very small lobes, barely there. His hair was black gray, receding at both corners and very thin. I share this hairline trait. His eyebrows were extremely thin too, almost absent, which made him look even scarier. His face was nicked up everywhere. There were scars around his lips, under his eyes, and across his chin and forehead. There weren't any big scars, nothing that would make you stop and notice, just little marks all over his face. It distorted his skin pretty badly, and up close with nothing but six-inch glass between us, you could see them clearly. It almost looked like he'd been stabbed hundreds of times in the face with a blade a quarter-inch wide and maybe a quarter-inch deep.

His arms were long, and his hands were big and thick. His nails looked manicured, surprisingly clean. His skin was pale. A gray white, like dirty paper. There was only a couple of strands of hair on his forearms, and his chest and neckline seemed almost completely bare, except for a handful of hairs down the middle of his chest. His left forearm was completely sleeved in tattoos, the biggest of which was a beautiful woman with horns. She was intermixed with skulls, flames, and words, although the words were indistinguishable.

He also had tattoos on that shoulder, about three or four of them randomly placed. There was a faded *W* tattooed on his pointer finger and an *L* tattooed on his middle finger.

On his right forearm, there was a word tattooed directly in the middle on the top, and about 4 or 5 smaller tattoos surrounding it, covering the sides on up to the elbow. There was a larger tattoo, another woman on his shoulder, and a bigger tattoo on his inner forearm.

He also had them all over his stomach, one down the side near his hip, on both breasts, and a big balance scale with a dollar sign about it. The scale itself was in the shape of a T and the dollar sign an obvious S. I later found out this is what they call a "stamp" in his gang, the Texas Syndicate, a segment of the Mexican Mafia. He said he was a high-ranking member, although he had to mouth and write out most of what he was trying to tell me on the window because he said people were listening on the phone.

He wore a two-piece short-sleeved white jumpsuit, but during the course of our visit on the second day, he stood up and lifted it to show me his tattoos. Nervously, Wayne looked around and whispered to me, not through the phone, but more like mouthing what he was trying to communicate into the empty space that surrounded him, "We'll have to be careful what we say because they listen to the phones. They'll hear our conversations, and I'm under investigation still, for gang shit in here."

His eyes danced all over the place, like a caged, fearful animal. He looked in every direction, then he settled on me, then shifted left and right again. I could see in the mirror reflections of people visiting and sometimes security guards walking behind me. I felt relief when he looked at the passersby because it gave me a break from the heaviness of his penetrating stare. He had a way of looking through me most of the time, and my inner self is a fragile and vulnerable place. It was the last place I wanted him to explore.

Twenty-Two

Every Coin Has Two Sides

*We can never judge the lives of others, because each
person knows only their own pain and renunciation.
It's one thing to feel that you are on the right path, but
it's another to think that yours is the only path.*

—Paulo Coelho

"I want to visit with you about my childhood and about my dad when you knew him. All I have are the stories people told me and the little I remember, although I don't remember Dad very well. The stories aren't good, Wayne, and in my head Dad and his family are cruel and violent people."

"I'm glad you came. I'll tell you the truth because you're blood, and for better or worse, you have a right to know. I don't want you thinking bad about your daddy, me, or the family, because it ain't always true the way other people see things. Sometimes people got one way of seeing things because they messed up in the head or something, and it ain't the truth like what they say. Every coin has two sides, boy."

With a desire to understand what I could from his perspective, I asked, "What was my dad like?"

He smiled. "Me and your dad was close. We were closer to each other than we were to anyone else. Anywhere one went, the other was there, like this." And he held up two crisscrossed fingers.

"We were tight; didn't no one come between me and your daddy. He got me out of trouble a lot, and I got him into trouble a lot."

He let out a belly laugh, and it startled me.

"You couldn't separate us, and all kinds of people tried. Especially them women. They'd get mad 'cause they couldn't get between us. Your daddy was a good man; he would give you the shirt off his back. I'm telling you, Stanley, you look just like him, and that's something you should be proud of. He was a strong man and a hard worker."

Again, I was overcome with a sense of pride. For all the anger and hatred I'd held so tightly for so many years, I couldn't shake the reality that I wanted my dad to be good. I wanted him to be a great man, and I wanted to look up to him. I needed a father figure I could see good in because it was the only way I would imagine ever seeing good in myself.

"He was happy when you was born, and that's why you're his namesake."

I needed to know if my dad related to me in a tender way, with any semblance of love and protection. I asked, "Did my dad love me, I mean really love me the way a father is supposed to love his son? Did he play with me, hold me, sing to me? You know, father-son stuff?"

"Yeah, he loved you a lot. He was so happy and proud when you was born."

I cannot express what it feels like to hear, for the first time, words that have been lost to you for 25 years. As a boy and even a man, I struggled with the absence of my father and the doubt of his love. The sound of this affection from someone so intimately connected to my dad didn't release me from the sense of doubt, but they were enough to send my thoughts reeling through the years of self-loathing because I'd never heard those words. Little boys need their fathers.

They need to know their fathers love them and care for them. With my dad out of the picture and out of my life, I battled questions about manhood, fears about being a husband, and dread about being a father. What do those things look like? Would I know how to be them? Would I have what it takes to be everything I wished my father would have been? There is such an extensive gap ripped in the heart of a boy when a father leaves and fails in his duties to tuck him in at night, to flirt with his mother in a loving way, to protect him from the monsters in the closet and under the bed. I'd always been aware that as a little boy, I needed my dad. Standing there listening to Uncle Wayne speak those words struck me with the realization that men need their fathers too.

I pulled myself out of such heavy thoughts and realized Wayne was referring to the letter I sent him during the process of setting this meeting up. He continued, "That picture you sent me of him holding you, that's how he was. He loved you a lot, and you looked just like your daddy when you was a baby when he was young. He saw you and knew you was his."

I felt a sense of pride rising again. I must have expected another answer because I was suddenly and unexpectedly overcome with relief.

"But what he was like?" I needed to know more about his personality—what made him who he was. I knew that would help me understand what made me who I was.

"Your daddy was pretty quiet; he didn't say much to too many people and never went out looking for trouble. Hell, neither one of us went out looking for trouble. It just always seemed to find us. It was like we couldn't do nothing without there being some kind of trouble waiting to get us.

"We would go out, and we loved it, you know, party, and we would be out having a good time, cutting up on the dance floor. And I guess other people in the bars would look at us and, you know, man, look at us and think we must think we're bad or something. And I guess they would try to show us we weren't as bad as we thought we were." He laughed at this. "We would just be having a good time, man; that's all, and we didn't care what other people thought, but if they came looking for trouble, we'd give it to them."

I was well aware of my own triggers and things that would set me off, but I wanted to know if I was like my father in this way as well. So I asked, "What would set you off?"

"I guess we'd always had a short temper, all the Leones, we learned it from Daddy, but sometimes it didn't take much to set us off. You know, you can walk into a place and see someone, and you know, man, you know right there you don't think too much of that person, and as the night goes on, if that person wants some trouble, you didn't like him anyway, and sometimes they could just look at you wrong, and you just want to go over there and slap the dog shit out of them. You know what I mean?" He laughed again.

We talked a while more about this type of stuff, but I could see he wasn't really going to tell me the entire truth, minimizing the violence of what they did and how they acted. What purpose would he have to be honest? He didn't seem to be able to take ownership of his own behaviors—doing what he'd always done and blaming others for their thoughts and actions. I knew he was trying to convey to me he wasn't a bad person, or as bad as it would appear—*locked up, handcuffed, in isolation, and segregated* in a maximum-security prison. Oddly enough he was very self-conscious about me knowing that.

"The only thing we was ever really guilty of was partying too much, and fighting was just a side effect of that. It was just what you did when you're out, and you don't give a damn about them sons a bitches. Sometimes you just have to slap the hell out of them! You know, man?"

We talked for what seemed like an eternity about the trouble they got into when they were younger. I was torn about how I felt listening to him. Part of me was repulsed, and as embarrassed as I am to admit it, very judgmental as I listened. Another part, perhaps the larger of the two, was proud, even with the twisted values and behaviors.

Something about hearing stories about my father intrigued me; his being the tough one or the one the girls like or the one who could save the day moved me. I was a little boy again, wading through the innocent

142

threats of childhood with the childish boasts like, "My daddy can beat your daddy up."

Introductions had been made, and the fears I brought into that prison were quickly taking their place behind my desire to *know* my dad. I was ready to probe deeper, willing to deal with the possibility of getting more than I could handle, and asked for more. "Tell me about your childhood and about my childhood, at least what you remember of it."

Twenty-Three

*The quality of our thoughts is bordered on all
sides by our facility with language.*

—J. Michael Straczynski

"There was a lot of us kids out there, man. You see, Daddy was married to his first wife before he met my momma. He had a whole bunch of kids with her: Joe, Ruby, and the others. He left that lady and got with my Alice, that's my momma. She was a lot younger than Daddy, but he always liked them younger. He was thirty-seven, and she was just eighteen. She was real young and purty. He laughed. My half brother Joe and the others was already older than Momma when Daddy married her.

"We weren't really close to Momma's side of the family; they were the white side, and I guess they didn't much approve of Daddy, man. Thought he wasn't good enough for her. They wanted Momma to marry someone better than Daddy, but Daddy was all right, man. He always had his own land and built his own house, and he told us we would always have a roof over our heads and food on the table. But he also let us know that if we wanted anything else, like partying and shit, that was on us. He let us go partying from the time we was ten, eleven, twelve, man, as long as we paid for it ourselves.

"I was going to the bars at eleven 'cause all my brothers had all been through there, so the bartenders, you know, they knew who I was, so they just let us in. I was drinking since I was little man, about this high." He leveled his hand to about the height of the chair he was sitting on. I scanned my eyes to follow his motion and realized with family patterns like this, my father missed on a huge segment of learning the proper boundaries and the responsibility he needed for a fulfilled life. None of them ever had much of a shot.

"Daddy, you know, he made that moonshine, that 'white lightning.'" He smiled. "And he would pour it in a little glass and set it on the table for us to drink. We didn't have to." I hadn't said anything about being forced, but this part contradicted the stories from other brothers. "He would just set it down, and we would take it and throw it back. Shit, we were like 5, 6, 7 years old.

"You got to understand, man, we was in the woods, man. Shit, the Wild West. Daddy built our little house, and there weren't many people in our little ole town, just a bunch of houses scattered with a dirt road down the middle. Everything was dirt roads in the fifties, no highways like you see now. And times was different when we growed up. It wasn't like it is today. Like this Obarama guy, shit, there wouldn't be no black president and no woman either. You just didn't put them in no office, you know; it was always the white man who was in charge.

"The town we grew up in was like that too. You know, the whites stayed in one part of town and then we had black town, where all the blacks stayed. Daddy use to put his big hat on, start to drinkin', and walk right down the middle of that dirt road with a gallon of his moonshine, callin' those niggas to come get their drink, man. He used to make a lot of money off them niggas; you know, keep 'em drunk all the time. That was some good shit. Daddy made some strong moonshine, man.

"We only had one sheriff in town too, and he wasn't in no uniform like you see now. He was just in plain clothes like you and me, you know, and he had this star he kept right here"—he patted his heart—"like you see in the movies and shit, man. And he didn't have no official car either. Shit, it was not until like the sixties, we had a car in town. He just rode up and down that dirt road on his horse. He had his belt and everything with that big ole pistol hanging at his waist. When I saw him and I was little, shit, I wanted to be like that son of a b*tch, man. I wanted to be a cowboy, ride horses, and shoot pistols, man.

"Your daddy wanted to be a rock star—Elvis Presley, man. He used to have this guitar too that he carried around for a long time. He could play too; he was all right, man. He got to where he could play a few chords on that thing after a while too, man. Yeah, he could play a few chords too, man. He couldn't sing worth a shit, but he got all right at that guitar. When we went partying, he would cut loose in them bars too, man, just up there, and we was acting like fools, didn't care what nobody thought.

"I guess that's why people didn't care too much about us. We would get in those bars, from about this big." He leveled his hand at his chair again. "And we would get to acting like fools, not giving a shit what any-one else thought. We was bad, man, and we ran the town. Shit, there was like twelve or thirteen Leone boys in town too, man. Daddy had a lot of kids, a lot of us boys, so nobody could say shit even if they wanted to. You messed with one brother, you got your ass whipped by ten of them, man." He laughed.

"Me and Stanley stayed together most of the time. It was me and him everywhere; when you saw one, you saw the other. Yeah, you never saw one without the other. The others would go out together, and we would, most of the time, me and your daddy, run out to the woods and spend the whole day out there. We wouldn't do too much, but the time would just fly, not like in here. Everything slows down in here, man. Everything moves fast out there, but when you get locked up in here, the world slows down and you got so much time, man. We would play Indians; you know, one of us would be a cowboy and the other would be an Indian, and we would chase each other and try to catch the Indians.

"One time when Daddy left, man, I went back into the house, and I grabbed his pistol. And I was holding it at Stan too, man, and he told me to put it down. And I told him it wasn't loaded, and he was telling me to put it down, man. And I don't know what happened. I had my finger on the trigger, but I don't remember pulling it, man, and that thing fired. I don't know how I missed him either, man; he was at point-blank range. But I missed him, man. Scared the shit out of me.

"We opened that barrel; you know, it was one of those guns where you could spin it and shit, and we opened it. And, man, that was the only bullet in there. I'm glad I missed, man. I don't know what I would have done if I would have killed my brother. I would have never forgiven myself for that shit, man." Wayne got really still and looked like he was lost in thought. I heard this story too, and Henry told me it was on purpose because Stan beat Wayne up in the woods. Wayne got mad and went back to the house to shoot Stan.

"One time, man, we went back about a quarter mile in the woods—all that land was Daddy's—and me and your daddy went into this creek where there was like a peninsula, man, you know, like a little island out there. We took these little trees, man, and we built us a fort out there in the woods, man. And we took all this brush and shit, man, and threw it on the top, and we made us a roof on it.

"We would sleep out there too, man, just grab a bag, and we was little but we would grab a bag of clothes and stuff and sleep out there in that little house, man. It would be dark out there too, and we would be like a quarter mile in the woods. And we would sleep out there by ourselves. And that floor would be hard as shit too, like sleeping in here. Yeah, me and your daddy was close, Stan; we was real tight.

"Sometimes, after coming in from the woods, we would come home, and Momma would be in the house, cooking dinner over an open fire in the house 'cause we didn't have a stove and shit like you do now. We didn't get electricity until somewhere in the sixties, man, Wild West shit, and all the kids would be sitting around. And Daddy would be over there with his moonshine. It was real nice sometimes too. It would be nine or ten at night, and it would get real dark out there. And we would all sit on that porch outside, the kids sitting around Momma and Daddy in their old chairs, and they would tell us stories too, man.

"Daddy would tell us about Grandpa Joe. Grandpa couldn't talk good English either, man. I met him once or twice when I was little, and he would try to talk to me, but then he wouldn't know what to say, and he would just start talking in his tongue"—Italian, I'm third generation in the States—"but Daddy would start talking about when he was growing up.

"He said his momma died when he was real young, and so his daddy raised him mostly by his self. Grandpa was a good man too; it wasn't like it is today. Today everyone makes a big deal if a man hits his kid. Shit, it wasn't like it is today, man. Daddy would hit us, and we didn't never think about it. It was normal; it was just accepted. Now they throw your ass in jail if you touch someone like that.

"Anyway, Grandpa and Daddy would get in fights about Daddy making moonshine—he did it since he was a little boy, man—and Grandpa would tell him he didn't believe in him doing that, so they would get in a fight. And Daddy said he would leave three or four days and come back, and Grandpa would be fine." He laughed again. "Shiiiit, man, that's just how it was. Yeah, we loved listening to Daddy tell those stories, man. It would be dark outside too. Momma would tell stories too. That's how they did.

"Daddy would tell a story, and then Momma would tell a story because we didn't have no TV or no shit like that, man. No, we listened to stories, and Momma would tell her stories, And she would scare the shit out of us too, man." He laughed. "She would tell us about this big black dog that would eat people, and she said he hid out in the forest and would wait there. Yeah, she would scare the shit out of us.

"Daddy would come home sometimes, and he would scoop me or your daddy up in his lap when we were little, man, and he would tickle us, And we would start wrestling with Daddy in his lap. He was good to us. All we had was us, man, and we was good to each other too. We'd go out drinking with Daddy sometimes, and we would look for someone to fight. And if we didn't find no one to fight, shit, we would fight each other, I guess so we could stay in practice, you know.

"We would get to fighting each other; that's how it was. We would be beating the shit out of each other, but if someone else came up and starting messing with one of us, whatever we was fighting over, we would let that shit go, and we would go from fighting one another to beating the hell out of this other joker. That's just how we were, man. We was family, and Daddy was all right to us. I guess he had a hard time when his momma died, but Grandpa raised him right.

"Daddy would let us party too, man. When we was little, he said he didn't care what we did when we were out there, but whatever we needed when we was partying, you know, we had to hustle to get whatever we needed. He said don't expect none of that from him. We always got a roof and food, but everything else we had to get on our own. We didn't do much out there, just drinking and partying, and when we got old enough, you know, eight or nine, something like that, we started looking at girls and shit. And we would get in competitions to see what girls we could get. Your daddy got some pretty girls, man, and we would take turns with them, you know.

"Shit, Stan would be with one girl, and then I would get with her the next week. We did that shit, man, you know; everyone dated everyone else's girl. Stan would date one, and when he was finished with her, I would say, 'Are you done with her, Stan? Are you sure?' And he would say yeah, and I would tell him, 'Because I want to get with her but if you're still with her, I'll stay back, man.' And he would laugh and say, 'I'm done with her,' and then I would be with her.

"We all did that shit, man. Daddy too. He liked them young; we liked them young. And I was dating this ole girl, and I got locked up. And she got to writing Daddy and shit when I was locked up, you know, looking for me, and she started I guess wanting my daddy. And he wrote to me and said he'd like to get with her, 'cause she's writing him and shit and telling him she wants to take care of him. I said, 'Yeah, Daddy, go ahead;

I was done with that bitch anyway,' and then Daddy got with her. You probably don't know this, but I was dating your momma first, before Stan.

"Yeah, I came across your momma, uh, Rose, first, in Louisiana. And she was over at the hotel, smoking a joint and drinking with me, and your daddy was there too. And this other girl was there. Me and that other girl got up and left to go smoke some more, and I came back three or four days later, and next thing I know, your momma and Stanley had done got together." He laughed again.

"Anyway, things wasn't always bad at home. Yeah, we drank and fought and damn near killed each other sometimes, but we was always there for one another. We was blood; I'd die for my blood. I'd die for you. If somebody out there wanted to hurt you, I'd kill them, or they would have to kill me. My blood flows in your veins.

"Momma was good sometimes and just not there other times. We was never too close with her. We would go off sometimes. If we were on a job or something somewhere else, we would write Momma, and she would be telling us to come back home, you know. And if we ever needed a place to stay, we could come back there and all. But then we would go back, and it was like she fricking didn't want us there. She wasn't really mean or nothing. She just didn't want us there.

"She would stay busy doing her own thing, and we would always be like, well shit, she acts like she doesn't want us here. Momma was young when she married Daddy, and he was hard on her. She was always trying to straighten up the place or cooking for everyone, but she really didn't have too much to do with any of us. She was there, but she wasn't around much.

"We're a distant family, Stanley. That's why it's good, why it made me feel so good to see you. Our family's always been distant, wasn't none of us too close. We had our groups, you know—me and your daddy, Henry and Joseph Earl, you know, the one who died—but we was never together as a group or nothing. I haven't heard from any of them in a long time."

I nodded, thinking to myself that saying their family was distant was as big an understatement as I'd ever heard.

"Your aunt Charlotte is the only one who came to see me. I don't know if you knew this, but me and your aunt Charlotte had a thing for a little while, you know, while she was with Henry, and I don't think Henry liked that too much. He came to see me once, but your aunt Charlotte kept wanting me to write dick letters to her, and I don't think he liked that too much."

I cringed at the thought of Aunt Charlotte and Uncle Wayne interacting that way. Again I was reminded that theirs was a family with no boundaries and no respect for one another. Never had I seen a group of people more ingrained in poverty than in that side of my own family.

"I got six kids with six different women, and I don't know a one of them. Yeah, I guess when it comes down to it, all you really got is family. That's why we got to stick together. Maybe if I would have stayed with one woman, you know, settled down a bit, and had myself some kids, maybe with Rachel, she's the momma of my first kid and a real good woman. She didn't go drinking, didn't go to the bars or nothing, and didn't want me going to the bars either. She was a Christian woman, and maybe if I would have stayed with her, my life would have been different. But we have to stick together. We're blood. My blood flows in your veins. You know what I mean?

"Your daddy loved you when you was a kid. You look just like him. In that picture you sent me of your daddy and you when you was a little one, the one where he's holding you and kissing you on the head, you look like him in that picture too. That's just what your daddy looked like when he was a kid. You're a mirror image of him"—I felt proud again— "and he loved you a lot. He would take you in his arms, and you would be looking him in the eyes. And he would throw you, man, high in the air. And you would start laughing. And he would catch you. Then he'd do it again and again, man, throwing you and you laughing."

It's interesting to me that my uncle's words could move me so deeply. I wanted my father to love me. I wanted there to be good memories, even if I couldn't remember them, because that would mean at some point in our lives he must have loved me.

"He loved to sit you in his lap, and he would start tickling you too. And you would laugh so hard you couldn't hardly stand it. Yeah, yeah, he would tickle you good. Your daddy loved you. He loved your momma too. He was real good to her too. He would come home after work, and he would tell your momma to sit down. And he would cook dinner for y'all, man. He could cook too. He would get in there and start singing and cooking dinner.

"We'd have a few beers, you know, just sitting back drinking, and your dad would be in there singing and cooking. He would sing songs to you too. Yeah, he would sit you on his lap and start singing those old Elvis Presley songs, and sometimes he would take out his guitar and start playing a few chords too, and you would just sit there and laugh and watch your daddy play."

I didn't remember any of what Uncle Wayne spoke about, but sitting there listening to him began to paint an entirely new picture of my father for me. It was the picture of a man I wanted for a dad. It was the image I'd had in my head when I'd thought about what I'd been missing as a child.

"Sometimes he would turn on this old record player they had too, and he would get the music all loud in those little apartments they use to manage, you know, over there in South Houston, and he would grab your momma up and start dancing all wild with her in the living room, turning her all around. And your momma would be telling him, 'Stop, Stanley,' and he would just keep telling her, 'Come on, baby.' And he would move her around, and they would start laughing and cutting up. Yeah, it was good times then too. He would get up in the morning early too; your daddy was a good worker, and he was real good to people too."

His words affected me greatly. I'd been told all my life that evil flowed through my veins. I was convinced that there was a curse on the Leone name, that somehow I was destined to be a manifestation of wickedness.

The images of my father dancing with my mom, laughing and enjoying one another was enough to cause me to doubt. I thought, *That doesn't sound like an evil man.*

"I was living in Louisiana before I moved into a little ole apartment where they were managing, and your daddy called me up and told me he would make me a partner in his business, split everything right down the middle, if I wanted to move to Texas, and he did too. Not seventy for him and thirty for me. No, he split it right down the middle, and he would get to laying tar in the morning, shingling roofs, and your daddy was strong. He would walk up this ladder onto a roof with a fifty-pound bundle of shingles in each hand.

"You kids would stay there with your momma all day while he was working, and she would take care of the apartments, you know, collecting rent and shit like that. And she would take care of you kids all day long. Your momma was good people. And when your daddy would get home, you and your stepbrother too—Johnny, he was pretty big by then, but your daddy loved him too—y'all would run to your daddy, and he would scoop you up in his arms and kind of burry his face in your neck you know. And there you were, laughing again."

Hearing about my brother Johnny, who was my half brother, not my stepbrother, and uncle Wayne's version of his relationship with my dad, only served to remind me that I was hearing a story of half-truths and lies. He was remembering things the way he wanted them to be, not the way they actually were. I have to admit it was easy to fall into his words, because they painted a picture of the way I wanted things to be too.

"Y'all had an old TV too, and your daddy would sit in his chair and watch TV with you kids until you fell asleep. He used to pick you up and lay you on his chest, you see, right here"—he motioned to his chest and neck—"and you would fall asleep the minute he picked you up. Those were good times. Your daddy was a good man. That's my broth—"

Uncle Wayne got real emotional. He had to stop talking because he was so choked up. It was one of three times when he referred to my dad as his brother and got choked up. All the other times, he referred to him as my daddy or Stanley, and he was fine. It was strange to see.

"I love my brother, man; that's my blood. We were as close as you can be. We couldn't be any closer; that's why I look at you and I think of you as a son, because me and your daddy were so close.

"Stanley and your momma used to get in some arguments, but don't let her lie to you; she would give as much as she got. They would get into it, and your momma would start to yelling and cussing, she'd tear him a new one, but that's all I ever saw. He never hit her or nothing like that as far as I know. I'm not saying he didn't; I don't want to lie to you.

"I know these other motherf*ckers want to lie to you and fill you up with stories like everything was bad, but I'm going to be honest with you, 'cause you're blood, you're my family, and you deserve to know the truth, so I'm going to tell you the truth. I never saw him hit your momma or nothing like that."

The anger rushed over my body like a tidal wave. I don't think Wayne noticed; he was so wrapped up in the storytelling. I jumped in to question him. "What about the time Stan bit my mom all the way around her neck, drew blood with every bite, to give her a necklace of bites? He told her he was the devil and kept biting her. I saw it."

He laughed. "Yeah, I remember that. He bit her good all the way around her neck."

That was all he said, and then he changed the subject. I let it go.

"He was a family man, more than me; he always wanted someone to keep with him. Not me, hell, I was too busy making them leave me or leaving them myself. Your daddy liked the thought of being with one of them. He was all family during the week, but shit, when we got paid, we'd get all decked out and party again.

"Me and your daddy had a pact, see, I told you, we had this pact with each other that we would party until we were fifty and then when we were fifty, we would, you know, get serious about life and settle down and have a family. I guess you have to take what you have at the time because you don't know where you will be at fifty, or if you will even make it to fifty, so I guess you have to get serious where you are. But we didn't know any better. We thought we would just party until we were fifty, and then we'd do all that shit, you know.

"We would get paid, and the first thing, man, your daddy would go to the kitchen and drink that Crown, you know, that was his drink, and we would go out for a good time. Your momma would get mad sometimes, and she would leave you kids at the apartment by yourself a lot of times—she would lock you in there and tell you to be good—and she would come in that bar looking for your daddy. And she would tell him to get his fricking ass home, and she would start all kinds of shit in the bar. I don't know; I guess she thought he was in there fooling with someone or something, but they would get into it right there in front of everybody because she wanted his ass at home."

He smirked again, like he knew some dirty little secret only he was privy to. I couldn't begin to imagine what stories, what mysteries of rage, pain, and deceit roamed through his head, keeping him company in his tiny cell.

"Yeah, your daddy would get into it with your momma sometimes, but he just slapped her from time to time as far as I know. I slapped the shit out of them sometimes too, but that's what you got to do sometimes when one of them bitches start talking shit, and I tell them, 'Get the hell out my face.' And they just keep on trying to make you look bad and shit, and they won't shut the hell up. And I'll give them every chance, and sometimes you got to slap the dog shit out of them from time to time. You know what I mean? I would tell them to get the hell away from me, and if they don't, then sometimes you know, you got to help them get the hell back.

"Do you like me? What do you think about your ole uncle here? Do you like me?"

The question caught me off guard, and I hastily responded, "Yes, I like you. I see some good things in you. That doesn't mean I don't think you wouldn't hurt someone if you had the opportunity, but I think in all of us there's good."

"I'm glad to hear you say that, 'cause they was saying, 'Your nephew hates you. He don't even like you. He won't even come back to see you 'cause he thinks you're shit; he hates you. He don't even like you.'"

I was confused about who he was referring to. I asked, "Who said that?"

"I don't know. I think it's these other damning inmates here. They're always talking shit to me, you know, trying to make me look stupid and shit, and I tell them to shut the frick up, but I can't do nothing, you know. I'm in this cell, so I can't get out and slap the shit out of them, but they keep on talking shit to me. They kept me up last night—I told you I couldn't even sleep last night because I was so happy you came here—and they were you know, making fun of me and shit, trying to make me fricking look all bad and shit, just screaming at me, telling me you wouldn't be back. Do you know anything about computers?"

"I know a little."

"'Cause I think they have a computer or something in my cell. I think they are spying on me or something 'cause I'll hear a voice like I'm talking to you right here, and I'll go over to my cell, and I look around, but I don't see nothing, man. I keep thinking how are they talking to me, but I don't see them anywhere."

"Do you think it might be in your head?"

"Yeah, I thought about that, if maybe I'm losing my mind or some shit, man, 'cause I can't figure out how they're spying on me. I didn't tell no one you were my nephew. How the hell do they know you're my nephew? You could have been anyone, and they know you were my damn nephew, man. I don't know how they're spying, but yeah, I thought maybe I'm losing my mind or something." He laughs.

My heart saddened a little to look at this man who was a part of my family and see him in such a miserable state. It must be a terrible thing to be locked away in a hole for the rest of your existence with the demons he created in his life. I asked him, "What do you fear the most, Uncle Wayne?"

"That you wouldn't want to see me."

"Look. I don't know much, but I do know when we're isolated from other people, we hear voices. I used to hear them when I was angry too, and most of the time, those voices are our worst fears. Most of them were lies though, see? I came to see you, and I like you, but a lot of times, we make those fears come true because we believe them so much.

"What I do when I hear those voices is pray. Even if I don't get an answer, I pray because it makes me feel better, because I'm closer to God in just the act of praying, and during those times what I need more than anything else is the same thing you need, to be connected to something."

"Yeah, I've read the Bible in here three times, page by page, from front to back. I can't understand most of it—there's so much contradiction in that damn thing—but I've read it."

"You don't have to read the whole thing. Just read about Jesus, and no matter who you read, no matter what book, his life is consistent. He was who he said he was all the time, even when people were making fun of him, running their mouths, trying to make him look bad, he was who he said he was. There are no contradictions in his life. Read that, and you'll understand the Bible. I don't care if you think he was the son of God or just some crazy, pacifist carpenter. Do what he does, and you'll be all right."

The security guard came and told me my time was up. I was breathing easy, and I felt disappointment to be leaving. I looked at Wayne, and he was tearing up. We stood, staring at each other, and he told me to let my mom and my brother, his namesake, know they could write him if they wanted to. He put his fist to the glass, I returned it, and we touched fists with glass between us.

He said, "I love you."

I said, "I love you too," and I meant it.

"I'll see you again, Stanley, and I know gas is nearly four dollars a gallon, so if you can't make the trip, maybe at least you can write me. I love you. We're blood."

I thought for a moment and replied, "I love you too, Uncle Wayne."

I walked out, and just before I stepped out of the unlocked door, I looked back. Uncle Wayne was standing there in his white jumpsuit, his hands disarmingly by his sides, hunched forward a bit, leaning into the glass, watching me go. He smiled and waved like a little boy who's grateful for the quarter he's just received. He looked sad. I stepped out the door, it locked in place behind me, and I looked back as the officers shackled and handcuffed Uncle Wayne in his little room.

I walked back into my life.

Twenty-Four

FAMILY TREE

Nobody can go back and start a new beginning, but
anyone can start today and make a new ending.

—MARIA ROBINSON

I left the Allred state prison with a heavy heart. I went there filled with hate and left completely empty. I didn't hate Wayne. I didn't feel sorry for him either. There is always a choice in life, and life is designed to reward us for the choices we make. If we choose love, we get rewarded with love. When we choose hate, I realize now, we get rewarded…with love. His reward is the same as mine, but his experience of it is different.

I thought about our meeting on the seven-hour drive home, and I processed through the many lessons I learned from Uncle Wayne. Some of them were obvious: Your experience in life reflects the choices you make. All of us have the potential for good and evil. Some of them, however, were complicated and caused me to question who I am. I began to reevaluate the definition I stamped on myself and tear down the prison walls I'd built around my heart.

They say you can look at the family line of an individual and see the stock they come from. That stock, oftentimes, can be a predictor for the type of person an individual is or will become. You can look at families as recent as the Bush family, three in politics and two presidents, or you can look as far back as the Bible, where the family lines are painstakingly charted in Numbers and each member of each line plays a significant role in the outcomes of all the others. My thoughts went something like this.

How's this for a family tree?

My grandfather on my dad's side was a violent, alcoholic bootlegger who, after the death of his mother in childhood, was raised by a hard father without the emotional care of a woman. He had more than twenty different kids with God knows how many women, a trend every one of his sons continued, including my father. He shot and killed one of his sons in a late-night fight and covered it up as a suicide. He burned down the house of his first wife because he wanted the land, married a woman who was nineteen years younger than him, having kids older than her, from time to time dated his sons' girlfriends, and eventually was shot to death for having an affair with another man's wife.

Let's branch off the tree along my dad's side.

I have an uncle who is a twelve-time convicted felon. He's admitted to me murdering at least one man, killing his unborn child while still in the womb of his pregnant wife, cutting his stepson's stomach open with his pocket knife, rape, burglary, being affiliated with the mafia, and being a drug addict.

I have another uncle who was murdered by his dad two weeks after getting into a car accident while drinking and driving. His newlywed wife was thrown from the car and killed.

Uncle number three went to prison at eighteen with a life sentence for statutory rape. He's living out the rest of his days on lifetime parole.

Uncle number four is serving two consecutive life sentences in prison for a double murder, where he brutally stabbed two victims to death and raped one, before and after. After meeting him in prison, I discovered he's more than likely developed some sort of schizophrenia, and I am almost certain he's bipolar. I'm not saying this out of judgment. I recognize the signs; I'm bipolar too.

My dad was an alcoholic, and by the time I was 5, I watched him rape, stab, almost shoot, and beat my mom numerous times a week. All this when he wasn't recovering from his drinking.

I have brothers I've never met call me from prisons in other states. I have sisters I didn't know existed reach out to me, along with their daughters and sons.

The branches on the other side of my tree?

My mom's mom had an affair on her first husband with my grandfather. She eventually left that man and married my grandfather, only to be left wondering who the father of my mom was. My grandfather never believed my mom was his and hated her before she ever took a breath.

He molested my mom until she was old enough to be taken further advantage of, when he began raping her for years, telling her she wasn't his daughter. As if this wasn't enough, he was also an alcoholic with violent tendencies, beating my mom while my grandmother worked. He eventually threw up his arteries—died from an alcohol-induced bleeding ulcer.

My mom's oldest brother is an alcoholic, although he is a kindhearted man. He's been faithfully married to the same woman all his life and has raised two children into adulthood. He is definitely the exception.

My other uncle is a pedophile.

My mom left home at fifteen, got pregnant and dropped out of school, and bounced around from man to man after that. She was used and abused by men from the time she entered this world, from her father up until her husband before the last, who was also a pedophile. She did eventually find a man who treated her decently, but he died a few years back of an alcohol-induced ulcer. Personally, my mother was broken, angry, and bitter. She thought being violent was synonymous with love. Oftentimes she could be physically and verbally violent herself.

Well, there you are, my family tree. What does that say about me? Nothing…all this time to discover that my family tree says nothing about me.

The beautiful thing about life is that it belongs to the individual and, ironically, only worth having if it is shared in relationships. Who I am is not determined by where I come from or who my family is. When I'm an old man, sitting on my porch, staring out into the open road, remembering the experiences of my youth, the adventures of early adulthood, and the love I experienced throughout, my life will not be a reflection of who my family was. It will only reflect how I choose to invest my life. It will be the fruits from this tree; the tree that grows from the seed I sow, that will be taken into account when judgment is passed and I'm held accountable.

Twenty-Five

LIFE IS BUT A SONG...WAITING TO BE PLAYED

As a man thinketh so is he, and as a man chooseth, so is he.

—RALPH WALDO EMERSON

I began to stir in my sleep as my body jerked a bit. As I opened my eyes, the flight attendant beckoned, "Sir, sir. I'm sorry, sir, but I'm going to need you to pull your seat back forward. Please. Thank you."

I can't believe I slept the entire flight. My dreams were so vivid. So fresh. Everything was so real, floating around in my head like music being blown about by the French horns and trumpets of the most beautiful symphony. It's amazing how the truth about what life is and who we are blossoms out of the mud and dirt that so often forms the realities we exist in. Three different meetings, three beautiful memories filled with insight and revelation into a past I've torn up and shredded my entire life.

There is a song, a soundscape, in which a piano plays, tiptoeing through the air in steady thumps of keys. It begins very lightly, slow and steady at first, baby-stepping along the path laid out before it. The keys almost whisper, peeking around corners, examining the rooms they fill, breathing lightly and ducking around corners, sliding up and down floor-length curtains, until finally they dance out into the open, slipping and sliding along the carpet in a graceful waltz, but never too long, always retreating into the cover of shadows, only to make its entrance once again.

The notes have found courage, and rather than sneaking about, timid and afraid, the thump of the piano grows louder and bolder, culminating in the grandest musical finale I have ever heard. I think about life, my life, and how this piece of music, this lovely work of art, is a metaphor for the path I have chosen. Circumstances crippled me in the beginning. I didn't know what was safe and what was dangerous. Rather than taking the time to discover danger, rather than risking injury, I tiptoed around perceived threats and hid behind curtains from lies and deceit.

I prayed that my thumps would be light, slow, and steady. I believed if my music was too loud or my melody too beautiful, it would draw the wrong kind of attention. So I lightly thumped my harmony throughout my life. As time passed I realized it wasn't so bad out in the open and that the music I make is quite beautiful, and magical, and I began to play a bit louder. I started playing freely.

The funny thing is, even with the awareness that my music was worthy of being heard, I still battled the fear of being found out, and although a steady increase in volume has constantly accompanied me throughout, just a small part of me watches through paranoid eyes, anticipating a bad note. Even when I play well, I worry, *Can I continue this? Do they like it? Does it really sound good, or am I just tone deaf?*

I have played beautiful music in my life. I have thumped quietly, and I have banged the keys, shattering all barriers and breaking all binds, only to recreate them and once again constrain my talents and abilities. What is this talk of music?

I have overcome physical abuse and violence. I have weathered the storms of homelessness and being destitute. I have been bloodied by rape, bipolarism, suicidal attempts, drug addictions, gangs, and felonies, but my head is still unbowed! I play beautiful music, and someday my culmination will consist of a healthy marriage, happy children, loving friendships, and the truth of who I am: an instrument meant to be played and heard.

I will play my music for all to hear, and the world will be more beautiful because of it. The world will hear my song, will dance to the melodies that massage their minds, and it will be a better place because I have added my song, a good song, to the symphony of this life.

Whatever the case, I rest in knowing I will reap the reward of love, just as each one of my family of trees, each of which has borne their own fruit through a lifetime of decisions, and the experience of that reward rests entirely on the decisions I make. I take solace in knowing the fruit I bear is not of bitterness, anger, hatred, resentment, and violence but of love, peace, gentleness, and kindness, and my reward will be experienced upon the feasting of the very same fruits I have borne. A bit wordy, I know, but it's the best way I know to express the complexity of feelings I have.

Twenty-Six

Closer than Ever

Do the thing you fear, and the death of fear is certain.

—Ralph Waldo Emerson

My plane landed, and I quickly headed to the rental-car station to get my car. The drive wasn't as far as I thought, but psychologically it was a 25-year journey away. Everything was surreal. The other vehicles seemed to pass by in slow motion, and I could see minute details on the faces of the men, women, and children in their cars. Gray-speckled goatees. A mole just below the left side of a woman's nose above her lip. A striped Polo shirt on a young boy and barrettes in a little girl's hair. I noticed details I am oblivious to in everyday life.

My surroundings were so rich, my senses so sensitive, even the ticking of my blinker seemed too loud to tolerate as I inched along the massive highways of California, switching lanes, attempting to speed my progress. It's the one time in my life I was comforted by the traffic, occupying my attention and relieving me of anxiety for the time being.

Wow. The traffic cleared, and I was on the open road, and so many thoughts raced through my head. *What will I say to him? What will he be like? I know he has kids; will they like me? Will he like me? How will I respond to him? Is he dangerous?*

Can I control myself around him? Am I angry?
What am I doing here? Why am I doing this?

All questions I didn't even know where to begin to answer. I've spent so much of my life swaying back and forth between trying to forget him and holding on to him. I guess I've always had a feeling that I could perhaps someday find him, but it always seemed so unlikely that I never really believed it. Now that the moment was approaching, part of me wanted to back out altogether, to turn around and go home. My experience has been that things, when left to the imagination, are often better than they ever are in reality. I struggled with the thought that I would be disappointed in meeting him and lose any of the good thoughts I had about him now.

Although the memories of him as a father were terrible, part of me still held to the possibility that maybe somewhere along the way he made some changes and was now, if not a good person, at least a decent one. The last thing I wanted was to get there, meet him, and realize he has made no changes at all. He didn't have to be Mr. Fantastic, but if he hadn't grown in any way, I didn't know how I would deal with it.

In spite of my fears, or maybe because of them, I did what I've always done and pressed on. Disappointment or not, I've waited too long for closure in this area of my life to turn back now. I gassed the rental a bit and thought about the positive words his daughter, my sister, I guess, e-mailed about him. He is her knight in shining armor.

He tucked them in and read to them at night. I let the thoughts wrap their arms around me, and I logged away every moment in memories I will replay a thousand times. The reality suddenly hit me that I was closer than ever to finding my father. A shudder passed through me, and I steadied my hands and continued on.

Twenty-Seven

Unexpected Welcome

Man cannot remake himself without suffering,
for he is both the marble and the sculptor.

—Dr. Alexis Carrel

I pulled into the neighborhood. The homes were very modest, and it reminded me of the residences portrayed in Snoop Dog videos. This was fitting since I wasn't all that far from Long Beach. Still, it was kind of odd to me, and suddenly this trip took on a comedic feel. The GPS said I was one-tenth of a mile away and that I should be there already. I made a sharp left and then followed the road around to the right until I was in front of what the GPS said was his home. I turned left and pulled next to an old work truck sitting in his driveway.

Getting out, I looked toward the house and made my way up the driveway. There was a steady hesitation with each step, and I felt like I was repeating the past with every foot I moved closer. Finally looking directly at the front door, I was seized by childhood memories and washed over with pain and sadness. I was 5 years old again, and it was the last day I'd see my dad for 25 years.

It all began before I got to the front door.

"No, Stan! Please stop!" Mom was crying.

The screaming triggered emotions inside me: anxiety, anger, disappointment. But what seized control was the fear I was suddenly paralyzed with, and all I could think of was finding someplace to hide. I heard his voice violently thrashing through the still air from inside the tiny apartment.

"What the hell do you think you're doing?"

There was the sound of slaps sliding slowly across flesh and banging coming from behind the door. Time seemed to slow down when Dad yelled, as though his voice commanded the very fabric of existence. At least my existence.

Hoping to avoid getting caught in the crossfire, I ducked behind my oldest brother through the front door and clung to him like static on clothes. We tried to hurry down the hallway toward our room when I saw a Hispanic man lying on the living-room floor, bleeding.

I stopped.

Back in reality I was overwhelmed with the memory. I was cautious and undecided. I didn't know if I could go through with this. I didn't think I could make it through. As I began to turn back to the car, the front door opened, and I saw a face looking at me through the screen door. It was a man with a scruffy beard and disheveled hair. The screen door flew open, and an old man hobbled toward me—in a hurry. I was defensive and spoke out.

"Dad?"

He didn't say a word. He was smiling, with sparkling eyes, and sort of crashed into me, gripping me in what was an awkward hug.

"Son? Son, I'm so glad you came."

It was my father.

His grip was strong, and he fell into me, burying his face into my shoulder. I'm in shock, and I half-heartedly put my arms around him to return the hug. This isn't what I expected at all, and I didn't know whether to be happy at his greeting or standoffish. What was the right response? Standing there, numb, I looked to the door and saw two young girls standing there, watching.

My sisters.

Dad let go of me, and I turned to face him. His cheeks shimmered in the light as streaks of wetness dug into his weathered face. He stepped aside, and Tiffany and Savannah both hugged me as well. They looked different from the three of us on my side of the family, but both girls had definite dominant Leone traits. Savannah more so than Tiffany, but still, there was an obvious Leone influence in both. Dad came up behind me and the girls stepped aside and escorted me into the house.

I know I should flood these pages with descriptions of what everything looked like—the girls, Dad, the house—but those descriptions seem so insignificant to me in the context of what I am experiencing and feeling. I will say this: Dad has lived a hard life, and it is evidenced in the severe limp he walks with, his sun-weathered face, and his calloused hands. The girls both have children and they are very young, not much more than teens. They are very sweet and Tiffany is definitely the quieter of the two. The house is, well, something to work hard for and be proud of.

I walked through the kitchen and was led into the living room, where Dad asked me to have a seat.

"I'm sure glad you came, son. It's been a lot of years. I can't tell you how many years I've waited for this day. I always wondered what happened to you and my other son, your brother, Cisco. Does he know you're here?"

"No one knows I'm here. I didn't know if I was going to come or not, and when I finally decided to, I had to move fast, or I would have changed my mind."

"Oh, well, I'm sure glad you did. I've waited 25 years for this day."

"I've waited a long time too."

"These are my daughters. That's your sister Tiffany, she's seventeen, and Savannah, she's eighteen. They're real close in age too, like you and your brother Cisco. I got seven daughters now; 5 of them were my wife's when I met her. She died 13 years ago."

Tiffany got off the couch and went into a back room with her son. Dad watched her go and then suddenly remembered something and shouted back at her.

"Tiffany, bring that picture of your momma and all you girls."

His voice sent chills up my spine, and I was thrust into the mind of a 5-year-old again, recalling pain from the past and opening old wounds. It was an odd sensation, recalling memories from the past while hearing my dad's voice in the present. Dad was talking, but I didn't hear a word he said.

I was used to his yelling. At the age of 5, I was even used to the blood. Dad made Mom bleed a lot. But this was different.

"No, Stan! He was just paying his rent!" my mom screamed. "Nothing else was going on! Please stop!"

I recognized this bloodied man as one of the tenants from the old beat-up apartments where we lived in South Houston. Dad was the manager, but Mom usually collected the money and wrote stuff down about who was where and who owed what. The man had come to pay his rent.

"Don't lie to me! You think I'm stupid?" Dad fired back.

I watched and listened in shock as Dad fired missiles at Mom, wounding her with each word that spit from his lips. Dad was the kind of person who used the f-word as a conversational filler, like "um" or "you know." It was at best vulgar, degrading, and bigoted, but it was the language of love he constantly beat Mom with. It was filth—like a mouthful of garbage he heaped on anyone he wanted to hurt. For him, these words were weapons. For me, they were a signal. They told me to get ready—somebody was about to get hurt.

Dad looked at the man slipping and sliding on the floor in a pool of blood. As he tried to get some sort of traction in the wet mess and failed, Dad screamed accusations at him that the man couldn't understand. He just sat there confused and disoriented. He spoke no English, and I didn't understand Spanish. He just babbled hysterical nonsense, and it scared me.

"No, no, no! Por favor! No, no!" His left eye was useless, as it seemed to struggle with the gaping hole beneath it and was swollen shut. Blood was spilling from his lower lip, and his jaw hung like clothes out to dry. He tried through tears to communicate, but the sounds of guttural nonsense only made things worse.

As he scrambled to get to his feet, Dad struck out at him like a viper lying in wait and extending itself at just the right moment to lock its lethal fangs into its prey. Just as the viper locks its jaw in a paralyzing grip, Dad latched onto the man by the hair. "You want to sleep with her? Don't lie to me! I'll kill you!"

"No, Stan! Just let him go!" Mom pleaded. "He didn't do anything! We didn't do anything!" Dad reached back with such fury it knocked her 5 feet in the air, where she tumbled to the floor.

It was eight o'clock in the morning, and Dad was drunk—again.

I was standing behind the kitchen door watching this scene unfold, feeling terrified and helpless. Dad was screaming spit-covered insults, holding the man by his hair.

Suddenly, in one quick but powerful motion, he slammed the man's face into an end table—the table next to the recliner where Dad always set his beer—sheering off one corner and crushing his face. The man screamed in agony, bordering on the edge of consciousness, and then went still.

I wasn't scared. As crazy as it was, I felt no fear at the act of violence itself. What terrified me was the prospect that Dad's power and wrath extended beyond my immediate surroundings. At the age of 5, there were very few things I could count as consistent in my life. What I had come to count on was the fact that Dad only beat us, and only in our home. He never hurt me when I was playing outside or when we were with other people. He never hit Mom when we were buying groceries or visiting Granny and Papa Cisco. Of course I was afraid of the anger and violence, but it was our way of life, and I knew how to survive it.

But this man, this stranger, shattered that belief. He had been terrified, sobbing, pleading. I couldn't understand what he was saying, but I recognized fear. I saw Mom wrestle with fear all the time. Watching someone else completely helpless, being pummeled by Dad, I realized there was no escape. My belief that I could run away from this life was an illusion. Maybe it had always been. This stranger showed me that Dad could hurt anyone, anytime, anyplace. The certainty of that uncertainty was paralyzing.

Dad left the man broken and bloody in the middle of the living-room floor and then turned to his next victim—Mom. She was lying on the floor, bleeding, sobbing, gasping, still pleading. He strolled toward her, scuffing his work boots along the dirt-covered carpet. *Whoooosh. Whoooosh. Whoooosh.*

"Stanley? Stanley, you all right?" My dad was looking at me oddly.

"Oh, yeah. I'm sorry. It's just been a long day. I'm a little tired; that's all."

The flashbacks were both unexpected and unwanted. Incidents that happened so long ago shouldn't have so much power and influence over me now. As I tried to clear my head, their grip tightened and choked the breath out of me. I was sweating. My mouth was dry, and there was a slight shake in my hand. Nothing had gone the way I imagined it. From the awkward hug to this moment, I was completely lost with what to expect and how to respond. It'd have to be all instinct from that moment on.

Twenty-Eight

BAD THOUGHTS

All men should strive to learn before they die what
they are running from, and to, and why.

—JAMES THURBER

I gathered my senses and realized Dad was still talking and they were waiting on my response.

"I'm sorry. I didn't hear you."

"You said in your video on the Internet, I guess in those presentations you do, that you played in the NFL. Is that right?"

"You've seen my videos?" I felt panic. My speeches were broken into three parts, and the first part, arguably the most violent and graphic, is all about him. I wondered what he saw and heard, and I wondered how he felt about it.

"Yeah. I did a Google thing—at least Tiffany did; I'm dumb. I don't know how to work no computer. She typed your name in, and all sorts of things came up about you, and I watched one of your videos on there. You said you played."

"No. I didn't play for the league. I went to a combine with IMG Academies in Florida and worked out with Ontario Smith and Byron

174

Leftwich. They're in the league. I did try out for the team that feeds into the Dallas Cowboys, the Desperados. I didn't make it though."

"I'm just excited I know someone who made it that far."

"Yeah, it was cool. I had a good time and learned a lot about myself too. It was tough going through all the workouts with those guys." I paused. "The house is nice."

"Yeah. When I heard you was coming, I had the girls clean up and try to make it look real nice for you."

He laughed at himself.

"I even had the guys in the crew I run come over and put down this new carpet. The other carpet wasn't as nice as this, so I had them come and do it for me."

I looked down at the carpet and was deeply moved. The carpet was new looking, and I could tell it was recently laid. The seam where two pieces were laid together cut right through the middle of the living-room floor, and although not perfect, it was the most thoughtful and meaningful carpet job I have ever seen. He had laid it for me.

We small talked for a while longer, and I quickly realized he didn't want to talk about anything that might make him look bad in front of the girls. I mentioned Mom and the stories I'd heard about him once, and he dismissed me, glanced over at the girls, and moved on to talking about the strip mall he maintained with the crew.

"They all work for me. I been there for a long time now, and the boss likes me. I used to do all the work myself, and didn't have as many men, but with this leg I can't do much more, so he let me hire some help."

"What happened to your leg?"

"I got shot when I was young."

"I heard about that. I actually met Henry before he died, and he told me about it." Dad's eyes got wide, and he quickly followed up my statement.

"Yeah, I was in the war. Did you know that? I was in the war, but I got shot while I was at home and got a dishonorable discharge. Yeah, that's when I got shot, during the war."

He was lying. He was never in the war. He got shot when he and Uncle Wayne tried to beat Henry up for money while they were drinking. I didn't say anything. It was too early to start rocking the boat now. Maybe later.

The girls talked for a bit, telling me about their kids and the deadbeat fathers. Both of them dropped out of high school and got pregnant by guys who were abusive in one way or another. From the looks of it, they were in for a tough life. No education and no inheritance makes for a difficult time supporting a family. Neither one worked, and they talked on about how boring it was sitting at home. Savannah had quite a personality and lots of energy to go with it. Tiffany was more of a deep thinker, and I discovered that she enjoyed writing poetry. Something told me she was probably pretty talented. From what I saw, she had a lot to write about. All in all, they were both very likeable, and I loved them right away.

Dad stood up, and of all things, I noticed his belt. Blood rushed to my head, and among the chatter from Savannah about being bipolar, I was ambushed by visions of a different dad than the man I was sitting with.

"Stan, please don't h-hit me. I'm s-sorry. I didn't do anything, baby. He just paid his rent. That's all he was doing! I swear to you!" Her eyes were wet pools of terror as he approached, his figure casting a sinister shadow over her petite body. He stood like a soldier staring down into the face of the dying enemy, and he felt nothing.

"So you still want to sit there and lie to my face, huh? I'll teach you to lie to me!" He took off his belt and wrapped one end of it around his hand, leaving the metal buckle dangling against the floor. I'll never forget how that dirty carpet seemed to hug and caress the weight of his belt each time it hit. Then, in a single moment, the buckle was torn from the carpet's embrace as he swung at her wildly and with great force, striking her.

"You better tell me the truth about what you do! I'm tired of you lying behind my back!" He swung the buckle again and again, biting into her face, head, back, hands—anywhere skin was exposed. She let out agonizing screams every time the buckle pounded her body and tore into her flesh. Then…he stopped. That's all. He stopped. His arm hung limp at his side. The buckle dangled inches above the carpet, bloodied from the carnage.

It's an eerie feeling to stand in the presiding silence that follows the chaos of drunken violence. I imagine it's like the calm before a storm, the deafening silence that warns of impending danger. In this case, however, the danger has passed, and the fury of the storm has battered and bloodied everything in its path. I stood there, and the silence was interrupted only by Dad's breathing and the slow, steady *drip...drip...drip* of the blood that clumped to the tip of that buckle.

Mom hadn't slept with the tenant. She was too afraid to even look in another man's direction. Dad taught her that early in their relationship when he blackened her face for looking out the passenger-side window at an oncoming car. There wasn't any fear to keep Dad from sleeping around, and it was pretty much the same thing for him every night—hitting the bars after work, getting drunk, and fooling around with whomever he wanted.

Mom knew what was going on—everyone did—but what could she do?

It was a vicious cycle that she didn't have the capacity or will to break. The only thing she could do was what she always did—anything to calm his fury. Usually this meant submitting to any and all his demands.

The silence ended, and Mom's cries pierced the calm.

"Please stop, Stan! You're hurting me! Please *stop*!" She curled up in a ball in the corner, covering her face, making herself as small as possible.

"Good! Die then! You deserve to die!" he shouted, driving home another blow.

He stopped again, letting the belt fall from his hand this time. Staring at something on the floor, he looked back at Mom with accusation in his eyes and then reached over and grabbed her by the hair.

"Look what you did! There's blood all over the floor!" he shouted, dragging her by the hair into the kitchen. "You want to bleed all over the place?"

"No, Stan. I'll clean it up. I'm sorry. Please, just let me clean it up!" Mom begged. "I'll make it good again. I promise."

Twenty-Nine

ABCs and 123s

There came a time when the risk to remain tight in the
bud was more painful than the risk it took to blossom.

—Anaïs Nin

"That's great, Savannah. I mean, great that you know you're bipolar. I didn't get diagnosed until I was 27. I mean, they told me when I was in the psychiatric center at 13 and put me on medicine, but I didn't stay on it. It messed me up pretty bad. They don't even make the stuff I was on anymore."

My body was there, but my mind and emotions were years away. I didn't want to remember these things. I wanted to make new memories, memories that were good. All my life I have carried the burden that I must have some wickedness within me if I came from a father as inherently evil as mine. But sitting there, watching Dad interact with his daughters, seeing how the girls looked on him with love, it was apparent to me for the first time that it was possible to make new memories to replace the old ones.

Dad stood again.

"I'm going out for a smoke. I'll be back."

"Wait. I'll go with you."

I nodded to Savannah and Tiffany—no doubt they would talk about me while I was gone—and stood up to follow Dad out of the front door.

"You know, I quit smoking. Started back up when I heard you was coming to see me."

He laughed again. There was a gentleness about him. He was quiet and humble. He had a way of sitting back and making you feel like he was listening to every word you were saying. He was hard on himself and insecure, but there was also a peacefulness as well. He was old, much older than his 60 years, and he struck me as a man who was resigned to the fact that his life was what it was.

I laughed back. "Don't start because I'm here. I don't want to be responsible for your smoking habit." I laughed again, but he was suddenly very somber and serious.

"You know, you was right. What you said in that video, about what I did to your momma, it was true. Probably all of it. I don't remember too much from back then. I was messed up all the time, and I guess some of it I just want to forget. Your uncle did shoot me. Shot me right here, near the hip. My leg's been bad for years and has gotten worse as time goes on. I got no feeling in it anymore from the knee down. I can't feel my toes. It's black and blue now too.

"The doctor says I need to go in for surgery, to get it right. I'll go in, just have some loose ends to tie up here first. But Henry shot me, trying to shoot Wayne. I grabbed that gun away from him and held it down—didn't know it was pressed against my leg—and he pulled the trigger. They rushed me to the hospital. I was bleeding a lot. Wayne and I had two ole girls in the car with us too, and they was screaming and scared."

"I knew Wayne did it. Henry told me what happened."

"Them girls don't know much about me before I met their momma. I never talk about it, just told them our family is not real close, that's all. I don't want them thinking they come from a family that's all messed up and crazy. I've been good to them girls."

"I understand. I can tell they love you a lot."

179

"Yeah. I was all they had. Just me and them girls. Their momma was gone all the time. Sometimes she wouldn't come home for weeks, and we wouldn't know where she was or if she was OK. I'd take them girls to work with me, set them up with some of the folks who worked the stores to look after them. They were always with me."

"Why was their mom gone so much?"

"Drugs. She was into the drugs real heavy, and she would get all messed up and be gone. I take real good care of them girls. A lot's changed; I've changed."

"What made you change?"

"Them girls did. When their momma died, I was a single dad with a four- and 5-year-old at home. I had to make a choice. I couldn't go out honky-tonking and drinking all the time with two little girls. I saw it like this: I give up my two girls—and I didn't want to give up my children; I already lost my two sons, you and your brother—or I quit drinking.

"So that's what I did. I quit drinking, and I started doing right so I could take care of them girls. I'm all they have. I don't know what they'll do if something ever happens to me."

"I'm glad you changed. I think it says a lot about how much you love them by changing something about yourself that wasn't good for them."

"I tried to find you boys. Your momma took y'all away. I didn't leave. She did."

"I don't blame her. She was terrified of you."

"Well, that might be true. But I tried to find you boys. I always wanted to be in your life, but I never could locate you. I'm sure glad you're here now. We got a lot of time to make up for. 25 years' worth."

"Yeah. We got a lot of making up to do; that's why you need to quit smoking again, so you can be here for a while! Don't you go dying on me yet. I just found you!"

We both laughed, and it was one of those moments you see on television between a father and son, bonding as one man to another.

"Well, son, we better get back in there. There's no telling what those girls are doing."

He threw his cigarette to the ground, and we headed back into the house. He entered first, and I followed, closing the door behind me. The girls were in the living room, shushing their babies, and I noticed something on the refrigerator out of the corner of my eye and turned to look at it. There are pictures hung neatly on the surface with a series of ABC and 123 magnets. I almost fell to my knees as my head began throbbing and the shushing of the babies got replaced with cries from my mother.

He thrust her against the refrigerator like a rag doll, and the magnets scattered. They fell to the floor like shattered glass, and the ABCs once used to hold our works of art in place—a bear I colored, a truck Johnny drew—were now dipped in my mother's blood.

I stood frozen next to the kitchen table, torn by my desire to save Mommy and the instinct to protect myself. She was so small and helpless, but all the desire in the world to protect her couldn't make me bigger than Dad.

So I picked up a dinner plate and held it in front of my face, believing in my childlike way that because I couldn't see them, they couldn't see me.

While Mom tried to prop herself up against the refrigerator, Dad began rifling through kitchen drawers. When he finally found what he was looking for, he pulled them out and laid them on the counter one by one.

Mom saw the steak knives on the counter and tried to run, but Dad reached out and grabbed her hair again, slamming her bloodied back against the refrigerator.

"No, no, no, Stan! You know I love you, baby. Please don't hurt me."

He pulled her head close to his face, drawing her ear to his lips. "Don't you realize that's what I want to do?" he said in a half-whisper, like he was sharing some dark secret with her. "I want to hurt you."

Standing up, Dad flung the knife with a downward flick of his wrist. It penetrated Mom's foot at the base of her toes, planting itself in the linoleum underneath like a toothpick in a sausage. She wept.

"Stan, you stabbed me! Oh God, please stop, Stan! Please! What can I do? Oh God!"

My stomach twisted into knots of rage and fear and pain. The image of Mom on the floor with a knife through her foot was too much for me to bear. I saw him standing over her, looking satisfied, as if it were a job well done. Then suddenly, all I saw was the color of rage—my own rage—fiery, red orange, and ravenous. My hatred for him consumed me. All I wanted to do was rip and tear at him the same way he had my mother.

But I was scared, and I did nothing.

Dad looked over and saw me standing there, tears pouring down my cheeks, sobs racking my small body. He let go of Mom and walked toward me.

His face, which just moments before had been stretched and distorted by drunken hatred, had fallen. He looked sad, in a desperate kind of way. Stretching out his arms toward me in an obvious gesture of comfort, I instinctively recoiled and shuddered.

I wasn't different from any other 5-year-old. I longed desperately for a father whose arms I could fall into—to be surrounded and protected from the big bad things of this world. The problem was, he was the big bad thing in my world. I knew in some way he loved me. But Dad's love was a toxic, poisonous kind of love. I knew in the end it was a love that could only hurt me.

Thirty

SOBERING THOUGHTS

*I may not have gone where I intended to go, but I
think I have ended up where I intended to be.*

—DOUGLAS ADAMS

"Stanley, you coming?"

"Yeah. I'm here. Just looking around."

"You thirsty or anything? Savannah, get him something to drink. You want something?"

"Sure. I'll take some water. Thanks."

"Savannah, make him a glass of water."

Savannah passed me on her way to the kitchen. I heard the refrigerator door open, and she called out, "You want something, Dad?"

"Yeah, bring me a beer."

Thoughts flooded my mind, and I was lost again in thoughts of who my father was when I hated him.

Ours was a house of alcoholic rages, rapes, and near murders. It was a house that felt safe when alcohol slept. Monday through Thursday was a different life altogether. When there was no bottle, Dad was just a man, a husband and father who danced with his wife in the kitchen and

183

fancied himself the next Elvis Presley. He was kind and thoughtful, and when strong enough to resist the lies of an impoverished reality, he did reveal the truth about life to us. I guess he made me feel special, even loved, but the pain he caused overwhelmed those memories.

When Dad started drinking, it was like a fog descended over our tiny little apartment, permeating everything and everyone in it, stifling the air, and choking the life out of us. The husband Mom adored and the father I needed would disappear inside the fog. Sometimes, unexpectedly, the fog lifted.

The sun would come bursting through the window, and I would get a glimpse of Dad again. He would sing and be silly with us, and there were smiles and laughter. But the fog never dispersed too far away for too long, and when it descended again, there was no trace of the good man to be seen. There was only the monster.

"You want a beer, Stanley?"

"Huh? Oh. No. I don't drink. I've had some bad experiences with it."

I knew it was a cheap shot, but I needed Dad to know I don't approve of the drinking and I'm not comfortable with it. It was absurd that he asked me if I wanted a beer. Beer, liquor, moonshine—it was all the stuff that destroyed my chance at a happy childhood. It ruined me most of my life. I started drinking when I was in the fifth grade, didn't get it under control until late in my twenties, and only now have a very cautious handle on it.

"It's late anyway, Dad. I'm going on 2 AM New York time. I'm gonna go and get some rest. I'll be back tomorrow, and we can visit more then. Tonight was an…interesting night for me. I have a lot to think about."

"All right, son. I hate you have to leave. We have room here, and you're always welcome. You can sleep here if you like."

"Thanks, Dad. I already have a hotel room, but that's real nice of you." I got up and walked to the front door as Savannah brought him his beer and me my water. I smiled, acted surprised, grabbed the glass, and gulped the water down. "I forgot about this. Might as well drink it since you fixed it! Thanks."

I hugged the girls, kissed the babies, and walked out with Dad.

"All right, son. I'm sure glad you came. I can't wait to visit tomorrow. Be safe going to your motel."

"Sure thing, Dad. It is nice to finally meet you too. I'll see you tomorrow." Dad reached out to hug me, and I had one last memory for the night. Eerily, the circumstances were exactly the same, but the context was different.

As he approached with outstretched arms, all I felt was revulsion. All I could think of was what he did to Mom. I didn't want him near me. I turned away.

I assumed his face changed again. When he lunged at me, knocking me into the wall and shattering the window above us, I was not surprised. I tried to cry out, but only the sound of air being expelled from my body came out as I hit the wall.

I'm not sure why Dad stopped there. Whatever the reason, he was done with me. As I lay on the floor half-conscious, he turned and walked back into the living room, flopping down on our old brown couch. I saw his face sink into the crack of the cushions, followed shortly by a rhythmic, raspy, growling sound—the familiar snore of a passed-out drunk.

The storm was over, at least for now. I looked across the kitchen floor at Mom, who was still sitting upright against the refrigerator in a pool of blood—in shock—staring off into space, saying over and over again like a broken record, "I'm sorry, I'm so sorry." I'm not sure who she was apologizing to.

The monster was sleeping, and we would be leaving soon. Again.

"Bye, Dad. See you in the morning."

Thirty-One

LESSONS LEARNED

Let your heart guide you. It whispers, so listen carefully.

—LITTLEFOOT'S MOTHER, *THE LAND BEFORE TIME*

I visited quite a bit with the family today. We laughed a lot, and Dad and I actually got to talk about some of the questions I had. I arrived late in the afternoon and decided I would take them to dinner. It had been a long night, and I slept heavily once I made it to the hotel and flopped into bed. I learned more about who my father is and was this second time around, probably because the awkwardness of a first meeting for both of us was gone.

I took them to eat at the Olive Garden, and that was an interesting experience. Dad looked uncomfortable from the time we entered. I noticed him looking around like he'd lost something once we were seated at the table. After asking him what was wrong, he told me he needed a napkin, but he couldn't find any. I reached over, unrolled his silverware, and handed him the napkin. He'd never seen cloth napkins before.

The one thing from dinner that got a bit uncomfortable was that Dad asked if he could order a beer. I was hesitant, experiencing a little

186

of the twisting in my gut but no flashbacks this time, so that was a good thing. I thought about it and told him to get whatever he wanted. Then he said to me that he wanted me to order one too. When I told him again I don't drink, he said that was OK and wanted me to order one anyway. The beers came, I toasted the family, and I set mine on the table. He set his next to mine. Neither one of us touched them during the meal.

At the end of dinner, Dad looked up and said it was the best night of his life, next to his children being born. He told me I made two of his dreams come true. First, he got to eat in a fancy restaurant, and that was something he never thought would happen. And second, well, he got to have a beer with his son, and that was something else he never thought would happen. It was a good night.

The girls told me about how good Dad had been to them over the years. They shared about late nights talking with him about their mom, him tucking them in at night, and even reading bedtime stories to them. They laughed when the subject turned to Dad's infatuation with Elvis Presley and pointed out the bushy chops Dad still wore. They were stories about a different man than the one I knew. A better man.

On my way to the airport, my spirit was light with joy. I was thankful for the opportunity to meet Dad, to rewrite a story that was discouraging at the least. I left with the realization that my father is a good man after all. He's not a monster; he's a little old man who's made many mistakes in his life and paid the consequences. We spent hours talking about what he would do differently if he could go back, and every one of the changes is noble and worth striving for.

I left with a different opinion about my father, about myself, and about my family. The reality is there is an ugly truth about families. Not all. But definitely some, like mine. Let me start with what I don't believe. I don't believe a mother cannot love her children. I don't believe a father cannot love his children. I don't believe people intentionally set out to hurt people.

What I do believe is there are things in life that hurt us, and sometimes we don't know what to do with it, so we perpetuate the pain by acting out in ways we're familiar with. It's an unfortunate thing, but dysfunction, once set in motion, has a tendency to cycle and intentionally imprison the very source that sets it in motion, in this case, my family. Dysfunction becomes an integral part of the life and lives of the families that themselves birthed it and creates for itself an environment in which it can survive. That environment is poverty.

Poverty is perhaps the most misunderstood disease in modern-day culture. Although not new in any sense of the word, poverty has become synonymous with being poor, and the problem with this misconception is, it is impossible to understand a problem if it is misdiagnosed. Poverty is so much more than simply being poor.

Poverty must be exposed for what it is and dealt with accordingly. My time with Dad and my uncles has taught me to examine the very nature of poverty: where it starts, how it lives, and how it dies. None of us intentionally set out to make mistakes and cause pain, but most of our problems are rooted in the ways we think, and it's our thinking that produces many of the problems we experience.

Somewhere down the road, my mother and my father's lives went terribly wrong. Whatever it was and whenever it was doesn't matter as much as the fact that their twisted perspectives of reality, this survival-based thinking, imbedded itself into their lives a long time ago and continues to destroy even now. Poverty must be understood beyond the pettiness of blaming individuals for behaviors that have come as a result of their thinking. We have to move beyond the symptoms of poverty and deal with the thinking that causes all the pain. Once we do that, poverty can be identified and overcome.

I am 38 years old. I have been able to overcome many things in my life. I have struggled with being poor and changed my thinking, and now I am comfortable and in control of my own destiny. I am a drug addict who hasn't touched a drug in 17 years. I am an alcoholic who doesn't drink. I was constantly afraid but changed my thinking and now spend all my time chasing courage. I've climbed 14,000-foot mountains, run marathons, competed in triathlons, parasailed, and stood on stage before hundreds of thousands of people and bared my soul.

I thought I wasn't smart enough, but I changed my thinking and graduated from Saint Xavier University as an All-American Scholar, an Academic All-American, and with magna cum laude under my name. I graduated with a 4.0 in my MEd program. With each step I take into the direction of this new way of thinking, I become more in tune with the truth of who I am, and the fruits of that truth reflect the desires and opportunities I have.

Despite all these accomplishments, none of which I would have achieved without the help and support of family and friends along the way, I am still burdened with the weight of a childhood I can't escape. I'm writing this to purge myself in part, and once and for all silence the lies of poverty that deceive me. I'm tired of carrying hurt that's not mine. I'm just tired. I want to free myself from the chains of poverty and pain that have had a firm grip on me, and *this* is the first step. Change your thinking, and you change behaviors. Change behaviors, and you change your life.

It is our duty, our responsibility, to use the faculties we have been given (our gifts, talents, and abilities) and those we have attained through trials and tribulations (perseverance, resiliency, and strength) to be a guiding light in the darkness of life for others who still struggle. There is a deceitfulness in abuse, drug addiction, and poverty itself, and others have to be willing to speak truth into the lives of those who are suffering.

It is not enough to know what poverty is. It is not enough to just hear a sad story. It is not enough to feel sorry for the less fortunate. It is not an honorable thing to stand by and feel empathy without being moved to action against what we know is wrong. My story is nothing if it does not move one to action, if it does not move one to love others through their hardships.

I'm tired of just words. I've done a lot of speaking about my story but it has caused less change than I would like. Words are powerful, but it is when words cause action that lives are changed, cycles are broken, and poverty is confronted. People need to begin speaking words of life that move us from poverty toward a better way of thinking. We must seize control over poverty. We must claim power over the lies of poverty, and actually do something about it.

Once we understand what poverty is and what it does to us, we need to begin rewriting our stories. These are new stories. Stories of faith, hope, and love. Stories of victory. We have to be willing to suffer for the betterment of our brothers and sisters, for to understand yourself requires a willingness to endure the impoverished thinking of others. Poverty doesn't dwell among us; it breeds within us. To assist those we love requires great sacrifice and an endless supply of patience and perseverance. It requires endless love.

I know there are kids who are going through similar experiences to mine—and in some cases the same or worse. Let my lessons with my family be a voice for you. I've learned that I can be better, that I am in control of who I am and who I am not, regardless of what happened to me, or who my family is. The same is true for each one of us. The power to define our lives, to write our own stories, is a gift that this life gives us. It is up to each of us to take advantage of that gift.

I've discovered that those who don't speak do have a voice. Those who disappear into the nothingness of survival-based thinking deserve to be seen. Those who've been beaten down can stand up. Let the truth of who we are lift your eyes to the mountains to witness the view that is promised to each of us.

I know there are adults who continue to live in poverty. People like me, who have carried burdens on weary shoulders so long, they don't know what life is without them. People who are so ingrained in poverty that to break the cycle is the most terrifying prospect they can imagine. People imprisoned by the illusion of despair, the viciousness of violence, and the trickery of poverty. It's time to open our eyes and truly see that we are not victims, but victors.

Poverty is a serpent that slithers in and out of truth and reality. It has a sly way of distorting truth and reality, painting one as the other. Life is composed of both truth and reality, but they are not the same. The truth is that each of us matters. Each of us makes a difference, and we are significant because we exist. To think otherwise is deception. It is simply wrong.

To experience a cool drink when you're thirsty, a warm meal when you're hungry, and a breath of air when you can't breathe is life. To hear the laughter of a child or feel the embrace of a loved one. The feel of grass under a barefoot, the chill of a cool breeze on a smoldering day. To see brilliant colors, taste delicious food, hear music that synchronizes with the very heart of the human soul is the natural state of our existence, and joys available to each one of us, regardless of race, religion, or economics.

The deception of poverty runs deep, and it robs life of its majesty, and replaces it with pain, suffering, and a sense of being less than. Poverty paints life with a different spectrum of colors altogether, and they are named extravagance, lust, gluttony, greed, apathy, despair, laziness, wrath, envy, pride, vanity, suffering, self-consciousness, and every evil thing. All colors designed to corrupt our thinking and convince us that we're something we're not.

The danger with poverty is that it becomes so ingrained in our lives that there is no distinction between poverty and truth. We're born into it and it is reinforced so violently and for so long that poverty becomes the only truth that a person knows. I grew up believing I was worthless, unlovable, and destined to hurt people. I believed that love was shown through abuse, that people were dangerous, and that life was a game of survival. It was such a part of who I was that to think otherwise wasn't an option. It's the same as not asking a question you didn't know was a question that could be asked. Does that make sense?

Mom and Dad were both born into this ugly world of poverty. In both scenarios, poverty passed, like a baton, from their hands to the hands of their children. It's in this context that poverty was passed to my parents and then transferred to me. But I see it for what it is, and no matter what has happened to me, I've come to recognize that poverty does not define me. I have changed the way I think, and the truth is simply that I am significant because I exist, and that people are worth loving. There is meaning to life. It is the truth for every one of us. We matter because we're here. My thinking is corrected, and I am finally enjoying the life I'm given.

This isn't to say the process of beginning to live is an easy one. There is a residual effect associated with the poison of poverty. The feelings of fear and the innate need to feel connected to someone safe was the dominant need of my childhood. My brothers and I clung to one another, often hovering together for protection. The sense of fear that shaped who we are as men crippled emotional and social development in all of us.

All three of us struggle with a fear and resentment of authority figures in our lives and have been plagued with chronic distrust of most male figures. There is a fear of success, believing that all good things end, often resulting in self-sabotage. Insecurities dominate our thoughts, never believing we are good enough, lovable, or deserving of a good life. We have all suffered with a longing to be connected in healthy, appropriate relationships with people who will really love us, accept us, and desire us to be successful. Yet there is an underlying belief that people are innately selfish and will ultimately hurt you that has to be identified and managed.

The questions ingrained in us that are the offspring of poverty are things like: Why weren't we good enough? Who am I? What does it take to be a man? How do I become a good husband or father? Can I be more than what they say I am? These are all questions we still struggle with on a daily basis, but they are lies we recognize and are determined to unmask. It's difficult—but not impossible. Where you're from has nothing to do with where you go. You are not who you have been. You are who you are today. If you don't like who that is, then be someone else tomorrow.

Life is not the doubts and insecurities that we struggle with. Those are things that prevent us from living the life we were meant to live. The longings for something more, to be more, to have more, to do more— are all desires that beckon each and every one of us to pursue it. Listen to it, and respond.

Through this process I have also learned that we need people. We need one another. No one can make it on his or her own, and we're not meant to. The only way for the plague of poverty to be exposed is for good people to engage in the fight and get involved at a deep, meaning-ful level in relationships with those who are in the arena now, fighting poverty. Helping one another is the only way to leave this world better than it was when we got here.

It is a long, rigorous process. It is different for each individual, and we should measure our effectiveness by where we are, what we have, and what we can do. Some can provide something as simple as a handshake or a smile, while others may offer a place to stay, or a ride to work. If each of us does what we can, we can make the world a better place a bit at a time. Doing what we can, when we can, and however we can, that is all that is required.

24030501R00113

Made in the USA
Columbia, SC
19 August 2018